How to answer *hard* interview questions

Other related titles from How To Books

Handling Tough Job Interviews
Be prepared, perform well, get the job

Be Prepared!
Getting ready for job interviews

High Powered CVs
Powerful application strategies to get you that senior level job

Management Level Psychometric Tests
Everything you need to help you land that senior job

How To Succeed at Interviews

howtobooks

For full details, please send for a free copy of the latest catalogue:

How To Books Ltd
Spring Hill House, Spring Hill Road, Begbroke
Oxford OX5 1RX, United Kingdom
info@howtoboooks.co.uk
www.howtobooks.co.uk

How to answer

answer

hard

interview

questions

*...and everything else you need
to know to get the job you want*

Charlie Gibbs

howtobooks

Published by How To Books Ltd
Spring Hill House
Spring Hill Road
Begbroke, Oxford OX5 1RX
Tel: (01865) 375794. Fax: (01865) 379162
info@howtobooks.co.uk
www.howtobooks.co.uk

How To Books greatly reduce the carbon footprint of their books
by sourcing their typesetting and printing in the UK.

British Library Cataloguing in Publication Data
A catalogue record for this book is available from the British
Library

ISBN 978 1 84528 238 7

Cover design by Baseline Arts Ltd, Oxford
Produced for How to Books by Deer Park Productions, Tavistock
Typeset by Pantek Arts Ltd, Maidstone, Kent
Printed and bound by Cromwell Press Ltd, Trowbridge, Wiltshire

NOTE: The material contained in this book is set out in good
faith for general guidance and no liability can be accepted
for loss or expense incurred as a result of relying in particular
circumstances on statements made in this book. Laws and
regulations are complex and liable to change, and readers should
check the current position with the relevant authorities before
making personal arrangements.

CONTENTS

I'd like to thank all those who have directly or indirectly contributed to this book by inspiring the questions, giving both great and terrible answers when I've asked them, or have simply been supportive during the creative process – that means you Julie Fry, to whom this book is dedicated.

PREFACE

We are now living in a world where changing jobs is considered a natural thing to do. Only a generation ago, my father being a prime example, it was common for people to clock up 20, 30, 40+ years of service with the one organisation. Most of us cannot conceive of remaining with the one employer for the vast majority of our working lives. It is a combination of the increase in individual aspirations and the nature of commerce which has brought about this change. The consequence is that practically all of us, whether by choice or circumstance, will be required to seek employment elsewhere and will need to go through the whole process of job seeking, applying and then being scrutinised in some way (the interview still being the most common example), before we can actually spend that first pay cheque.

I will briefly cover the search and application process, however the main thrust of this book is the employment interview itself.

It's getting on for twenty years now that I have been fortunate enough (some might say unfortunate enough) to be on the side of the desk where sits that scariest of dragons: the interviewer. During that time I have seen candidates who have inspired me to almost offer them the job there and then and not let them leave the building until they've signed a contract. I've seen candidates excuse themselves to go and throw up due to nerves. I've seen candidates who have tried to convince me that they were doing me the greatest favour in the world by deigning to come for interview. I've seen candidates whom I've thought were mute, such was their reticence. I've seen candidates whose vocabulary ranged all the way from 'yes' to 'no'. I've seen candidates who gave me such detailed answers to my questions that I was on the verge of losing the will to live.

The sheer variation of quality in the performance of interviewees has prompted me to distil what I've learned into one manageable body of advice which, I hope, will give you the edge when it comes to getting that job.

What follows are my tips on how to prepare for the interview itself, how to conduct yourself at the interview and, most crucially perhaps, examples of the kind of answers we interviewers REALLY want to hear. These are grouped into categories known as 'competencies' as the approach most modern organisations take these days is the 'competency-focused' interview. After all, we, as professional managers, are trying, on behalf of our organisations to secure the services of the most wonderful, motivated, efficient and productive employee, while trying to show how clever we are at recruitment at the same time!

The interviewer(s) are never the enemy. They may use methods which you think are in turn obvious, brutal or downright devious, but remember it is all in the cause of getting the right person for the job who will fit in because of their skill set, personality and attitude – for cultural fit is really important in terms of the likely longevity of their term in post. One day you may very well be sitting where they are and I'll bet you will be able to justify your approach for the cause!

Finally, if you have been asked a particular question in the past that stumped you, or you are anticipating a question that I haven't covered in this edition, you are welcome to email me your question and I will personally give you a considered response. Send your question to: charlie.gibbs@live.co.uk.

I hope you will find this book useful and I wish you every success in your chosen career.

Charlie Gibbs

Chapter 1
FINDING THAT JOB

While the intention of this book is to provide you with great answers to tough interview questions, it would be remiss of me not to at least touch on the subject of job-hunting. After all, you either need to be actively looking for and applying for jobs or be the subject of a headhunting exercise before you can stun them with your carefully crafted answers!

Job vacancies fall into two camps: those that are advertised and are made available to the public (either the internal population of an organisation or the public at large) and those which are sometimes known as 'hidden vacancies' – those which are given to recruitment agencies, headhunters and the like, or those which are not yet advertised but you have made a speculative application for.

Did you know that it has been estimated that only around 15 per cent of available vacancies are actually advertised in newspapers or magazines? Newspaper advertising costs are verging on the prohibitive for many organisations these days. Even small-circulation, provincial newspapers can charge several thousands of pounds for one-off adverts in the 'situations vacant' section, so many employers are turning to alternative media such as the Internet. There are many well-known job sites in the UK such as TotalJobs.com, Reed.co.uk, Monster.co.uk etc. Most job sites will also allow you to register your search preferences and then e-mail you when jobs matching your selection criteria are posted.

However, many employers still like to place adverts in specialist publications such as trade and professional magazines in the hope that the specialist readership is more likely to elicit a greater response than the pot luck that is generic press advertising. Choose where you search for your next job carefully.

OK, so you've now seen an advert that has caught your eye and you are sure you want to apply. Firstly, does the advert say that applications are to be made by supplying a curriculum vitae plus covering letter or via application form? Lets look at some pointers for dealing with each of these.

Filling in your application form

- Once you receive it, take a copy or two of it to draft your responses. You will want the form that your prospective employer to receive to be immaculate and not have any blots, rubouts or scribbles on it!
- Read all the instructions contained upon it carefully and comply with them.
- Do not be tempted to try to put a form through your computer printer and have your typed words line up into the boxes – it will take you forever!
- Never, ever, EVER write in any of the boxes 'See enclosed CV.' It is a guaranteed way to have your application rejected. Employers use these forms for a reason; they do not take too kindly to someone who is too lazy to be bothered to fill them in.
- Boxes on application forms tend to be small. Choose your words carefully. If the box simply is not big enough for what you want to tell them, attach a piece of plain paper with your script and refer to it on the form.
- When listing your previous employers, ensure there are no unexplained gaps.
- Try to adopt a positive attitude throughout the form. Stress achievements if you can.
- If you are asked to name referees, ensure that you have sought their permission first, or if you do not want them contacted until you've been made an offer, indicate this on the form.

- Once you are happy with your draft, transfer the detail to the original form. Always write application forms in your neatest hand and in black ink for preference as this photocopies well. Never use any other colour except black or blue inks.
- Once you have completed the form, photocopy it for your own records. You may wish to take it to interview with you to refer to.
- Draft a covering letter to go with your form. Keep it brief and always use the term 'Dear Mr Smith', or whatever the recruiter's surname is. Don't be tempted to use their forename, even if the advert has it on, as this is over-familiar. Never write 'Dear Sir or Madam' as it too demonstrates a lack of attention to detail.

Curricula vitae

I will leave it to you to decide on the style and content of your curriculum vitae. There are many sources which will advise you on these aspects. Here are some brief pointers:

- Use the best paper you can afford.
- Use only white or off-white paper.
- Do not use a fancy hard cover or binder.
- Use a simple font such as Arial and use the same font in your covering letter.
- Never use a generic covering letter. Be specific in its content by bringing out one or two elements of how you match what they are looking for. It is not just a wrapper for your CV!
- Your CV needs to get past that first 30 seconds after the recruiter has picked it up. Imagine yours is just one of 50 or 60 or more applications received. You want your professionalism to stand and not stand out because you've used bright yellow paper!
- Stress your achievements in your CV; not simply list your past employers and job titles.
- Comply with any instructions in the adverts such as supplying your current salary – you may wish to do this within your covering letter.

Imagine your delight, constant reader, when two weeks later you receive on lovely headed paper an invite to attend an interview for this potentially wonderful new job! That's when your hard work really begins. In Chapter 2 I will explore what you need to be thinking about before you actually attend the interview.

CHAPTER 2

PREPARING FOR THE INTERVIEW

Unlike preparing for a sporting event, you can never over-prepare before you go for an interview. You will never 'leave your game on the training ground'. Think of each minute you spend in preparing as an investment in your potential career. To use a well-worn phrase: 'Fail to prepare, then prepare to fail'.

When should I start preparing? Assuming that you did at least some preliminary research when you first decided to apply for the job, as soon as you receive the letter inviting you to interview! In order to prepare properly in terms of research on the organisation and analysis of yourself, you need to set aside time where you can be focused and free of interruptions.

You would be extremely lucky to attend an interview completely unprepared and sail through by a combination of your sparking personality and incisive wit (which no doubt you DO possess).

Remember, there are no second chances, no retakes in a real-life interview situation. You have to be on top of your game and be prepared to respond to questions you may find difficult and to talk about yourself in highly personal terms. This is not the time to hide your light under a bushel! The reality is that this is a selling exercise. You are selling yourself from the moment you submit that application form or post your CV.

ASSESSING YOURSELF

Before you even embark on your journey of securing that fantastic job, it is advisable to take stock and do some self-assessment. In understanding what you are looking for in a job you can develop clear goals and targets to assist you. You shouldn't enter into looking for a new job frivolously. This is a potential life-changing decision after all!

There are many factors which may influence you reaching the decision to either begin work or change job. Maybe you feel you have not had the breaks you deserve this far. Maybe you've been overlooked in the past for promotion or development. Maybe you think circumstances are not right for you to have the job you want. I'm with George Bernard Shaw on this one, who said:

> People are always blaming circumstances for what they are. I don't believe in circumstances. The people who get ahead in this world are people who get up and look for the circumstances they want; and if they can't find them, make them.

PERSONAL RATINGS AND COMPETENCIES

What follows is a simple method for assessing your strengths and weaknesses and also those skills known as 'transferable skills' or 'competencies' which are skills you acquire as you meander through life. They may be consciously acquired or gained by osmosis. Either way, these are not job-specific skills, but ones that can be readily applied to different roles. Incidentally, the word 'competency' has generated a lot of heat and light over the last few years within the world of human resources and indeed the interview which you attend may be described as a 'competency-based interview' or a 'competency-focused interview'. In either case, what they mean is they will be asking you questions aimed at finding out whether or not you have the competency level in the areas they require rather than simply seeking confirmation of the information contained in your CV.

Have a look at the descriptions of competencies listed below.

Competencies tend to fall into broad categories such as those described below.

Drive for achievement

Defined as: *The individual grasps opportunities to achieve and exceed their business and personal objectives; success is a great motivator for them; desires to perform tasks to the highest standards; is generally positive and enthusiastic at all times; does not suffer too greatly by setbacks and is tenacious; is resourceful and self-driven; can accept change and is flexible; has a high level of energy; leads by example.*

Strategic thinking

Defined as: *The individual can think about their industry/sector as a whole; can identify threats and opportunities to the organisation; can monitor the progress of short- and longer-term projects; can manage multiple priorities; understands the link between departmental and organisational objectives; recognises the interaction between people and technical issues in achieving objectives.*

Relationship building

Defined as: *The individual puts effort over a sustained period of time in building influential relationships; puts effort into building both external and internal relationships; understands the importance of good business relationships; demonstrates proactivity in utilising the expertise of others; works with others to formulate solutions; builds on friendships and actively networks.*

Commercial awareness

Defined as: *The individual understands how organisations work; can apply commercial and financial principles; demonstrates an active interest in the financial performance of the organisation in terms of profit and loss, cash-flow, added value, routes to market, competitiveness, etc.*

Leadership of change

Defined as: T*he individual works with others to implement change; helps to clarify and avoid ambiguity; willingly accepts change; takes responsibility for driving things forward; can identify and initiate change; understands the interconnectivity of departments and how change affects others.*

Leadership skills

Defined as: *The individual demonstrates an ability to share a sense of vision and common purpose; has respect of others through words and deeds; inspires loyalty and commitment; has an adaptable leadership style depending on individuals and circumstances; can create and build teams; is inspirational and enthusiastic; demonstrates empathy; can transform strategic objectives into firm actions.*

Continuous improvement

Defined as: *The individual demonstrates the ability to identify the actions needed to make things happen in a quality-oriented way; can ensure these actions are carried out; seizes opportunities to make improvements; establishes conditions to ensure continuous improvement; can plan and organise tasks; can challenge the status quo.*

Customer awareness

Defined as: *The individual can demonstrate an ability to meet and exceed customer expectations; recognises the prime importance of the customer;*

can anticipate future customer needs; goes the extra mile for the customer; takes responsibility for developing long-term relationships with customers; forges partnerships that contribute to future growth opportunities for both customer and own organisation.

Decision-making skills and judgement

Defined as: *The individual can demonstrate a readiness to make high-quality decisions based on the information to hand using logic and analytical skills; breaks complex issues into component parts; considers the outcomes of varying courses of action; can draw reliable conclusions from disparate and often conflicting sources of data; can make sound decisions in a timely manner; is able to make decisions with an awareness of the political climate internally.*

Influencing skills

Defined as: *The individual demonstrates competence in convincing others or impresses them in such a way as to gain acceptance, agreement or behaviour change; sets a positive example by modelling behaviour; has excellent listening, oral and written communication skills; has the ability to influence peers, subordinates and superiors and key decision-makers; can influence at tactical and strategic levels.*

Development of self and others

Defined as: *The individual demonstrates an interest in the development of others as well as himself; seeks out opportunities to learn new skills; encourages others in their development; accepts coaching and mentoring responsibilities; monitors own and others' skill levels; keeps abreast of development in their chosen field.*

Teamworking skills

Defined as: *The individual demonstrates an ability to work cooperatively and productively with others; copies the teamworking styles of others;*

*looks for opportunities to work in ad-hoc and established teams;
understands how to set and monitor team objectives and goals;
recognises the differing skill sets of individuals and the need for a mix
within teams.*

LEVELS OF COMPETENCE

Interviewers will often have already defined the levels of competence
the potential jobholder will need to possess in each of these categories
prior to the interview. Their ideal candidate will score above the
minimum level against each particular competence. However,
interviewers also live in the real world (hard to believe, I know) and may
recognise that they are unlikely to find someone who straightaway
exceeds their minimum requirements. More often than not, the
candidate who has the highest overall score will be the one that
receives the offer. The fact that you may score lower on one or more
competencies does not necessarily mean that you won't be offered the
job – an enlightened employer will then build training into your
induction period which will address these shortcomings.

Which level of each of these competencies do you currently possess? It
is easily understood that someone can be 'OK' at something or 'brilliant'
at something in everyday life. But how do employers stratify the level of
competence an individual has? Many organisations have gone through
a long and painful process of examining their competencies and putting
into words what each level of competence looks like. Below is a typical
example of the type of analysis that has been done in the 'real world'.

TASK

Get a piece of paper and a pen. Read through each competency level description in turn and write down which level you believe you are operating at currently. Once complete, you will have created a fairly comprehensive Competency Profile of yourself. This process is an excellent way for you to focus your mind on what skills you actually have. Once you have a self-awareness of your skills, this will enable you to speak so much more eloquently to your prospective employer. I have rated these levels 1–5, with 5 being the highest.

Drive for achievement

Level 1 – is motivated by success and the desire to perform tasks at a high standard.

Demonstrated by:
- Shows the desire to perform tasks to a high standard.
- Is driven to achieve excellent standards.
- Is enthusiastic and adaptable.
- Displays high levels of energy.
- Enjoys working hard.

Level 2 – is positive and enthusiastic generally; is resourceful and proactive.

Demonstrated by:
- Often makes suggestions and recommendations.
- Is not phased by setbacks or new challenges.
- Displays a flexible and proactive approach to work and achieving objectives.
- Regularly uses own initiative.

Level 3 – can accept change and is flexible and applies sustained energy in order to adapt to new requirements.

Demonstrated by:
- Can articulate the need for business change to move the business forward.
- Creates an environment in which peers and subordinates can achieve challenging objectives.
- Remains positive in the face of setbacks.
- Seeks to find answers, not problems.

Level 4 – displays tenacity in the face of unforeseen circumstances and difficulties.

Demonstrated by:
- Understands internal politics and interpersonal sensitivities and differing agendas.
- Takes on enthusiastically new challenges and tasks.
- Is an effective planner and maximises the use of everyone's time who is involved.
- Goes above and beyond what is needed to get the job done.
- Is not afraid of taking calculated risks.

Level 5 – Models drive and resilience and leads by example.

Demonstrated by:
- Is single minded in achieving objectives.
- Is driven by objectives and targets the majority of people could not deliver.
- Tracks the progress towards the achievement of objectives.
- Displays passion in their role.
- Demonstrates commitment to the company and acts as an ambassador at all times.

Strategic thinking

Level 1 – strictly speaking, there is no level 1 competence in this competency.

Level 2 – understands greater organisational context, markets and competitors.

Demonstrated by:
- Understands relationship between own role and business strategy in the short term.
- Can interpret some business strategy in the terms of operational plans.
- Uses customer feedback to make improvements.
- Gives some consideration to external factors.

Level 3 – can maintain an overview of complicated situations with an eye on detail.

Demonstrated by:
- Sees beyond the immediate needs of their own area to understand the interconnectivity of departments.
- Has an eye on the future at all times.
- Maintains an overview of complex situations but controls the finer details.
- Understands the impact of strategies on the medium to longer term.

Level 4 – sets plans and objectives with a view to the future success of the organisation in terms of technical and people issues.

Demonstrated by:
- Understands the impact of strategies in the long term.
- Has cognisance of people issues.

- Embraces and works with technological advances.
- Recognises trends in performance in both the organisation and it's competitors.

Level 5 – Translates short- and long-term decision-making into actions.

Demonstrated by:
- Actively contributes to the strategic direction of the organisation.
- Is inspirational and engages others with the organisation's vision.
- Can utilise all specialisms in achieving organisational goals.
- Can provide solid business rationale for large expenditure.

Relationship building
Level 1 – makes efforts to build and maintain a network of internal and external contacts.

Demonstrated by:
- Uses others to complete tasks.
- Responds helpfully to requests for information.
- Is courteous and honest in dealing with others.
- Is aware of own impact on others.
- Keeps others informed of own progress in work.

Level 2 – understands the value of building up sound working relationships.

Demonstrated by:
- Puts sustained efforts into building relationships.
- Uses both formal and informal channels to communicate with others.
- Checks understanding when communicating.
- Can identify key decision-makers.
- Is aware of the importance of including the right people at the right time.

Level 3 – is highly proactive about getting others involved.

Demonstrated by:
- Demonstrates diplomatic skills and is tactful.
- Recognises cliques and alliances and can utilise these.
- Recognises others' talent and utilises it.
- Can read 'body language'.

Level 4 – with others, constructs solutions, building on their ideas.

Demonstrated by:
- Encourages suggestions from others without being judgemental.
- Takes on board criticism.
- Can overcome traditional organisational barriers using novel solutions.
- Facilitates the efforts of others.
- Develops relationships which facilitate the resolution of complex problems.

Level 5 – regularly uses the cooperative and combined efforts of others to add value to the results.

Demonstrated by:
- Builds an influential presence in the external business environment to raise profile with key customer groups.
- Represents the organisation's interests persuasively with key stakeholders.
- Is proactive in keeping a network of contacts across the industry or field.
- Attempts to build symbiotic relationships with others external and internal to the organisation.

Commercial awareness

Level 1 – shows a level of interest in internal and external business issues.

Demonstrated by:

- Finds out about how the organisation works.
- Knows who the organisation's competitors are.
- Knows who the organisation's main customers are.
- Seeks to develop general business knowledge.
- Keeps up to date with current affairs.

Level 2 – can analyse in terms of profit and loss, cash-flow and added value.

Demonstrated by:

- Understands basic financial and commercial terminology.
- Keeps abreast of current business performance.
- Keeps abreast in terms of product and market development.
- Understands how own role/department contributes towards business success.
- Is aware of cost implications and their effect on the bottom line.
- Seeks to maximise productivity and reduce costs wherever possible.

Level 3 – knows the marketplace, competition and business issues faced by the organisation.

Demonstrated by:

- Has sharp operational focus so that actions can be prioritised and put into context.
- Fully understands the business plan and can communicate corporate objectives.
- Understands key messages from the profit and loss report and balance sheet.
- Knows the position of own business in terms of market share.

Level 4 – focuses on profitability and contribution to increase competitiveness.

Demonstrated by:
- Capable of managing cost or profit centres.
- Uses commercial judgement to enhance growth opportunities.
- Can assess market trends and has the capability to make decisions which will enhance organisation's ability to compete.
- Understands the underlying issues affecting the performance of the business or organisational unit.

Level 5 – applies financial strategies and tactics in the wider context.

Demonstrated by:
- Understands acquisitions, mergers and divestments.
- Develops creative new financial and commercial strategies to enhance growth.
- Confidently communicates messages from company financial documentation such as profit and loss accounts, balance sheets, etc.
- Benchmarks against others in order to seek commercial advantage.
- Uses external sources to keep informed of competitors' actions/developments.

Leadership of change
Level 1 – can successfully adapt to changing conditions and circumstances.

Demonstrated by:
- Endeavours to be resilient in situations which may appear unclear or contradictory.
- Shows a willingness to broaden skills and try alternative work.
- Understands the need for progressive change.
- Can adapt quickly and successfully to change.
- Assimilates new ways of working well.

Level 2 – enjoys the change agenda and willingly accepts the need for change in methodologies, materials, workflows or technology.

Demonstrated by:
■ Understands how change supports the vision of the business and links with business strategy.
■ Anticipates and plans for change in own function.
■ Actively cooperates in implementing change.
■ Demonstrates an awareness of the 'big picture'.
■ Sees change as a positive thing in respect of career-enhancing skills.

Level 3 – identifies ways to improve the organisation and encourages others to do the same. Takes on responsibility for driving the change agenda.

Demonstrated by:
■ Can articulate the benefits of change and shows confidence about taking on different tasks and activities.
■ Works well within a continuously changing and improving environment and helps others do the same.
■ Leads change with vigour and enthusiasm.
■ Can produce own innovations and is prepared to take risks with new ideas and concepts.
■ Supports people through the emotional impact of change.

Level 4 – frequently identifies and initiates change affecting specific organisational operations.

Demonstrated by:
■ Prepares and implements plans for the changes taking into account the material and people factors necessary to make the implementation work.
■ Conducts changes with an eye on minimising disruption to outputs and quality.

- Manages and anticipates the consequences for those outside and inside the organisation.
- Works closely with subordinates, peers and superiors to integrate change activities.
- Takes the time to get to know what people really think about the changes and allays these fears where possible.

Level 5 – understands how change drives towards the achievement of the business vision and strategy and can manage complex change programmes.

Demonstrated by:
- Manages the expectations of key stakeholders such as customers and shareholders effectively at all stages of the change process.
- Leads dynamically organisational change.
- Maintains a powerful motivating vision for all affected by change and encourages a positive approach at every level of the organisation.
- Maintains an overview and focus on the change agenda to ensure it is happening.

Leadership skills
Level 1 – in deeds and words, gains the respect and confidence of colleagues.

Demonstrated by:
- Able to give guidance and support to colleagues.
- Gains the confidence and respect of the team and supports them in achieving targets.
- Clearly communicates individual and team goals.
- Generates plans instructions and directions.
- Continually reviews progress and gives clear and specific feedback.

Level 2 – can build teams, involve others and motivate them.

Demonstrated by:
- Demonstrates integrity and trust in dealing with others internal and external to the organisation.
- Is able to maximise the performance of others.
- Anticipates conflict and takes steps to resolve this at the earliest possible stage.
- Defines tasks clearly, including objectives, outputs, timings and available resources.

Level 3 – inspires loyalty and establishes credibility quickly, motivates and enthuses.

Demonstrated by:
- Celebrates and rewards successes with colleagues and teams.
- Adopts a coaching and mentoring style with subordinates.
- Delegates effectively to encourage skill development.
- Is accountable for the organisation's policies, agreements and procedures.
- Is committed personally to the organisation's vision.

Level 4 – handles situations involving people with confidence and is empathetic. Develops a leadership style that empowers others to constantly achieve and exceed personal and company objectives.

Demonstrated by:
- Talks beyond today, about future possibilities optimistically.
- Shows others how they can benefit and contribute to the business.
- Takes personal responsibility for the team/department, representing them and their interests to the business.
- Displays flexibility in leadership styles in order to tell/sell/involve and delegate.
- Communicates inspiringly to wide audiences.

Level 5 – contributes to the strategic direction of the organisation and has influence over behaviour at an organisational level.

Demonstrated by:
- Can steer through complex political situations effectively.
- Establishes goals and gives others freedom and accountability for achieving these goals.
- Acts as a role model to all of the leadership and brand values of the organisation.

Continuous improvement

Level 1 – completes tasks within the allotted time and with the correct quality.

Demonstrated by:
- Pays attention and challenges processes and content.
- Typically gets things right first time and within timescales.
- Plans own time and resources to meet the tasks ahead.
- Can prioritise work in order of importance and urgency.

Level 2 – can challenge the status quo and generate new ideas.

Demonstrated by:
- Searches for new solutions to make required improvements.
- Challenges current working practices in order to identify areas for improvement.
- Can manage multiple tasks to meet a goal.
- Adapts own working practices to meet new requirements.

Level 3 – knows how to plan and organise tasks.

Demonstrated by:
- Good at mapping out processes in order to get things done.
- Can use resources such as people, materials, machinery, etc. effectively in order to achieve targets.

- Understands key performance indicators and knows how to measure against them.
- Understands how to combine or separate tasks in a workflow.
- Sets daily, weekly, monthly and yearly targets.

Level 4 – grasps opportunities to make improvements and sees them through.

Demonstrated by:
- Is able to identify existing processes and suggest improvements.
- Recognises duplication and opportunities for integration.
- Gets rid of as much red tape as they can.
- Understands both the tactical and strategic picture.
- Encourages others to challenge the status quo and to suggest improvements.

Level 5 – creates strategies that lead to process improvement and longer-term business planning.

Demonstrated by:
- Develops products or services that stay ahead of competitors' efforts.
- Plans for the longer term.
- Recognises and champions the need to work 'smarter' not 'harder'.
- Brings in on time and within budget large projects.

Customer awareness
Level 1 – understands that the customer is important to the organisation. (Note: 'Customers' in this sense can mean internal as well as external customers.)

Demonstrated by:
- Recognises the importance of internal and external customers.
- Treats every customer respectfully.

- Complies with organisation's brand values.
- Can utilise customer-care skills effectively.
- Spots potential problems and resolves them before they reach the customer.

Level 2 – identifies customer needs and responds appropriately.

Demonstrated by:
- Displays a positive attitude when dealing with customers.
- Responds quickly and with respect to customer requests and informs them of progress.
- Can negotiate a positive outcome with customers.
- Has refined questioning technique to clarify customers' needs and expectations.
- Researches customers for ways to improve the service offered.

Level 3 – anticipates and responds to changing customer expectations.

Demonstrated by:
- Recognises the cost/benefit implications of providing the service or goods.
- Identifies a range of solutions which exceeds customer expectations.
- Actively suggests improvements to make the customer experience better.
- Establishes empathy and rapport with the customer.
- Benchmarks customer satisfaction levels.

Level 4 – develops long-term relationships with customers and establishes personal relationships with key players.

Demonstrated by:
- Can adopt the perspective of the customer and understands their needs, wants and expectations.

- Seeks first-hand customer data and is able to utilise it well.
- Meets with peers regularly to assimilate their experiences with customers.
- Looks for symbiotic outcomes with customers.
- Recognises service which is above and beyond what is required.

Level 5 – forges strategic partnerships that enable inputs to business opportunities.

Demonstrated by:

- Shows that the customer is at the core of decision-making.
- Understands the bigger picture and communicates this to others.
- Sets customer-focused strategies and objectives.
- Promotes a customer-focused culture.
- Is a champion for excellence in service and enthuses others to be the same.

Decision-making skills and judgement

Level 1 – analyses issues and breaks them down into smaller parts before coming to a decision.

Demonstrated by:

- Thinks through outcomes before acting.
- Can learn from mistakes.
- Generates a range of solutions and challenges existing practice.
- Assesses all the available data and refers to others before making decisions.

Level 2 – considers and takes responsibility for the impact a decision may have on others and in relation to business success.

Demonstrated by:

- Understands when the decision needs to be referred to others.
- Makes decision within their own authority boundaries.

- Uses established procedures to ensure correct action is taken.
- Makes high-quality decisions in a timely manner.
- Can make decisions without complete information.

Level 3 – draws reliable conclusions from disparate sources of data.

Demonstrated by:
- Gives consideration to how decision impacts on others.
- Deals with unusual problems confidently without hesitation.
- Does not put off making a decision to avoid conflict.
- Does not put off a decision to avoid 'getting it wrong'.
- Considers the cost implications to a decision.

Level 4 – makes timely and sound decisions when data is less accessible, inconclusive or contradictory.

Demonstrated by:
- Not afraid to take risks to find a solution.
- Seeks a practical solution despite vagueness of data.
- Can assess multiple or complex or contradictory data in order to reach decision.
- Understands cause and effect.

Level 5 – can take decisions which require political or organisational interpretation with an eye on internal politics but which are beneficial to the organisation.

Demonstrated by:
- Evaluates the relationship between short-term consequences and long-term gains.
- Is persuasive when presenting case to stakeholders.
- Is confident about making decisions which involve the organisation going forward into uncharted territory.

- Is not afraid of controversy and will make decisions with cognisance of the political landscape.
- Is often sought out for advice by peers, superiors and subordinates.

Influencing skills
Level 1 – behaves in a straightforward and transparent way that sets a positive example.

Demonstrated by:
- Wins respect and influences others by own behaviour.
- Is confident and determined.
- Sets a positive example.
- Encourages others to challenge and does not mind being challenged.
- Communicates clearly both orally and in written form.

Level 2 – is aware of the impact on others, is a clear communicator, speaks and writes clearly, is a good listener.

Demonstrated by:
- Regularly shares own views in a clear manner.
- Can articulate the key points of an argument.
- Can be assertive when working with others.
- Observes and listens and understands what is being said.
- Demonstrates integrity when dealing with others at all times.

Level 3 – has the personal stature and capability to influence a broad range of people including key decision-makers.

Demonstrated by:
- Displays a variety of styles of action from diplomatic to assertive.
- Uses the appropriate approach to diffuse difficult situations.
- Is able to compromise when necessary.
- Identifies key influencers and focuses on their requirements.
- Demonstrates clearly confidence in all communication scenarios.

Level 4 – adapts style and interacts at all levels, whilst maintaining credibility, to secure commitment.

Demonstrated by:
- Identifies the key influencers and focuses on their requirements.
- Can compromise in order to achieve agreement seen as benefiting all parties.
- Uses appropriate influencing, assertive and negotiating techniques to diffuse difficult situations.
- Can persuade senior colleagues by being confident and assertive, and sensing best timing to gain most favourable outcome.
- Radiates experience and self-confidence in all communication situations.

Level 5 – influences at individual, team, departmental and corporate level.

Demonstrated by:
- Can deliver organisational messages confidently and with conviction.
- Keeps abreast of sector developments to influence external and internal customers.
- Understands completely organisational politics.
- Has strong lobbying skills.
- Can influence at all levels within the organisation.

Development of self and others
Level 1 – knows own career path and actively works towards achieving career objectives.

Demonstrated by:
- Has a positive mental attitude and seeks to be professional at work.
- Contributes fully and seeks additional responsibilities.
- Seeks goals for self and looks for learning opportunities.
- Identifies opportunities to develop and support colleagues.

Level 2 – markets self and others for opportunities for development; recognises others' career aspirations and supports them.

Demonstrated by:
- Regularly asks for feedback on own performance.
- Is aware of what is required to achieve career ambitions.
- Gets actively involved in developing others.
- Does not prevaricate and makes things happen for themselves.
- Consistently tries to develop current skill set.

Level 3 – continually improves the capability of the organisation through contributing to a learning culture.

Demonstrated by:
- Gives practical feedback to others.
- Mentors and coaches others to achieve their full performance capabilities.
- Takes direct accountability for success or failure of subordinates.
- Sees the appraisal system as an excellent way to identify training needs for self and others.
- Ensures training needs analyses results are acted upon.

Level 4 – actively addresses career development and pushes for the achievement of career plans.

Demonstrated by:
- Is pragmatic about one's own strengths and weaknesses and how best to get the results needed.
- Gives practical guidance and support to others in achieving their career ambitions.
- Recognises more subtle talents in others and actively encourages the development of these talents.
- Conducts the appraisal process in a professional and thorough manner.
- Looks for opportunities to 'stretch'.

Level 5 – measures and monitors skill levels throughout the organisation with an eye on future needs.

Demonstrated by:
- Keeps abreast of developments outside immediate area of expertise.
- Makes sure others get the resources they need to deliver what is expected of them.
- Is intuitive about people; takes informal and creative risks with them.
- Maximises the potential of the organisation's human capital.
- Strives to be an employer of choice by demonstrating commitment to people development.

Team working skills
Level 1 – is an effective team member.

Demonstrated by:
- Works effectively with others in a team.
- Requests help, or offers support when required.
- Cooperates with other team members and has a flexible and open-minded approach.
- Projects a positive image of teamworking.

Level 2 – Develops effective and supportive relationships with colleagues.

Demonstrated by:
- Draws on each team member's particular talents to maximise the effectiveness of the team.
- Contributes to the running of the team.
- Shares ideas and data with team members.
- Can work across team boundaries.
- Aware of the strengths and development needs of other team members.

Level 3 – understands how and when to set team objectives and utilises the talent of all team members.

Demonstrated by:
- Able to capitalise on the strengths of team members.
- Makes use of everyone's innate abilities.
- Recognises the cultural aspects of teamworking.
- Is a champion for diversity.
- Defines success as when the whole team contributes and shares in the glory.

Level 4 – looks for opportunities for inter- and intra- teamworking to achieve bigger business goals.

Demonstrated by:
- Can put personal needs aside in order to concentrate on team needs.
- Suggests ways of teams working together to achieve business goals.
- Suggests formation of new teams to satisfy the needs of particular projects.
- Can identify factors which hinder team performance.
- Strives to assist the team in developing its own identity.

Level 5 – models teamworking and champions the benefits of partnerships across the business.

Demonstrated by:
- Acts as a role model for others.
- Can use 'blue sky thinking' to circumvent hindrances to effective teamworking.
- Encourages a sense of *esprit de corps*.
- Is inspirational and morale boosting.

Phew! Quite a list, I'm sure you will agree. It can be quite cathartic to go through this exercise. The information you glean from doing this will not only give you a general sense of what your competence levels are at this moment in time, but it can also advise you when you are revising the content of your curriculum vitae. Perhaps some of the terminology I have used here has caused you to think 'Yes! That's exactly what I do!' If so, I'm glad. Use these terms to expand on your role and responsibilities detailed in your CV. It is often difficult to find a form of words that fully describes what it is you do exactly. I'm sure there are some phrases here you can adapt for your own use.

RESEARCHING THE ORGANISATION

An obvious place to start preparing for your interview is to research the organisation you'd like to work for. There are many, many sources from which to gain the kind of information you need, ranging from the Internet to periodicals, annual reports, etc. All of these have their own part to contribute in building up the picture you have of the organisation.

The Internet will obviously give you access to the organisation's own website. However, be aware that the organisation will use this medium to present the face to the world that they want, and it may be heavily 'spinned'. Putting cynicism aside for a moment, make sure you read as many of the web pages as you can and jot down salient points as you come across them. You will often find information on their markets, their products, their employee numbers, their green credentials and usually details of how you can contact them directly.

For larger companies, call up their public relations department (it may have many other titles) and ask them to send you any brochures or literature that they have all about the company.

Now most employers will have expected you to do at least a basic Internet search on them and I've lost count of the number of times a candidate has recited verbatim statistics published on the website. To many of us, this is lazy research. Unimaginative and predictable. I will expand on this in Chapter 6 on questions and answers later on.

So what should you do? Using what you have gleaned about the organisation as a starting point, see if you can find out who their competitors are and what they have to say on their websites.

It is much better to answer an interviewer in response to the question 'What do you know about us?' with a brief summary of what you've learned followed by your own question such as '... however, I see that Company XYZ is also expanding into the Pacific Rim market in direct competition with yourselves. How do you see that battle going?'

It is a golden rule when researching or collating data on any subject not to suffer from 'paralysis by analysis'. You must react to what your research tells you.

EXAMPLE

You are going for a job with a company which manufactures parts for the production of cigarettes. Your research tells you that you the company has enjoyed growth over the past 20 years and shows no sign of declining. However, the recent introduction of anti-smoking legislation in the UK has made you think that this company must be doing something right in order to continue growing. You dig around some more and find that in the UK smoking is actually in decline through a combination of the new legislation and through greater awareness of health issues by the general public. Ergo, the only reason the company can still be growing is because they are selling outside of the UK.

You do some more searching and find that the world's growth markets are India, China and other 'developing' countries. Now, it is tempting to then just drop into your conversation with the interviewer your knowledge that these are the growth markets. How much better does it sound when you come out with: *Are there any plans then to expand your manufacturing operations into China and India to give you a more direct route into the growth markets?* This not only lets your interviewer know that you are aware of where the growth markets are, but also that you have thought through what it might mean to them as a company.

The Annual Report is an invaluable source of historical information on an organisation as it reflects the previous year's trading/activities.

The Annual Report is often a daunting read as it contains highly detailed financial information. My advice is that unless you are familiar with financial terminology, simply scan those pages. The juicy stuff is contained in the Chairman's Report (usually near the end). This is the narrative report to shareholders by the top person in the organisation on how the previous year has gone. It will also point out where the organisation hopes to be going in the future. This again is valuable information you can take with you to the interview.

TIP

Companies which are public limited companies (PLCs) are duty bound to supply copies of the most recent Annual Report to anyone who requests one. Find out the registered address of the company and telephone their Public Relations Department for a copy.

Lastly, but not least, how much information on the post you are applying for is actually contained in that job advert? Not much, I'll wager. Enough to capture your interest, sure, but enough to decide whether or not this really is the job for you? Probably not. Telephone or e-mail the Human Resource Department and ask them for a copy of the formal job description. This should have much more detail than the advertisement and again provide you with clues on how to prepare.

TIMING IS EVERYTHING

There is an old saying relating to appearing for an interview: *If you are not ten minutes early, then you are ten minutes late*! Do you know, it's true!

If you are way too early it may appear that you have (a) not researched the travel time; (b) are a tad desperate to impress; (c) have poor time management skills. Be aware of potential road traffic issues if you are travelling by car and make sure all public transport selections will have you arriving in plenty of time. Take along with you the original invitation letter which will give you the organisation's telephone number should you have to call ahead and explain that you are going to be delayed. If you do not have a mobile phone, make sure you have change for a payphone.

Ten minutes is almost 'respectful'. It allows the organisation plenty of time if they have not finished their preparations just yet and you are the first candidate.

It may well be that the previous candidate's interview is extended a little or they are late in seeing you. However fed up you are at this obvious personal slight, please do not let it show on your face! Remember, you might just be grateful for the interest you have generated in them whereby they don't notice the passage of time and your allotted time runs on!

PLANNING WHAT TO WEAR

It's time to head for the interview and you have one question: what is the dress code?

Should you be strictly formal? Should you just go ahead and be yourself? After all, they won't want to employ yet another worker bee, will they? What about earrings, nose studs, tattoos, etc.? Should they come off? Would you make more of an impression if you stood out from the rest of the crowd?

Dressing for the interview is a big issue and many get this woefully wrong. The answer is actually very simple. The job interview is a formal meeting between people who are assessing each other's capability and suitability to work together in a professional environment which could lead to a legal formal agreement between an employee and employer – the employment contract – therefore its not overstating the case to call it professional. The dress code then must obviously be biased towards the formal.

Prepare for it with all the seriousness it requires because you need to create an impression on those whom you are meeting that you are a responsible and resourceful kind of a person.

This means that the casual look or even the smart/casual look is out. It means that the conservative (no, that doesn't mean going for the David Cameron or John Major look, I meant with a small 'c') look is what you need to work at. Even if you are going for an interview as a call centre operative who has no contact whatsoever with the public or a part-time summer job, it will surely make a difference if you go to the interview dressed formally. One rule that most human resource people promote is that an applicant must dress as if he or she is going for the interview of a job one level higher than the post actually being applied for.

The point of dressing yourself well is to leave behind an impression of yourself as well groomed and professional. Nothing does this as much as the clothes you wear, the fragrance you wear and the colours you wear. With conservative colours and clothes you are in the safe zone with most people whereas a daring fashionable look could just disqualify you for too much attitude of the wrong kind.

Some of the things for female applicants that are to be avoided are:
■ too much jewellery – remove any visible piercings except discreet earrings;
■ brightly coloured clothes or nail polish;
■ chewed, unsightly nails;
■ skirts that are too short and clothes that are too tight or revealing;
■ accessories that are too colourful or floral;
■ Inappropriate shoes (leave those killer Jimmy Choos with the four-inch spikes at home);
■ collarless shirts, etc;
■ strong perfume.

And for guys:
■ pale coloured suits;
■ suit, collar and no tie combo;
■ rolled up sleeves;
■ tattoos on display;
■ overpowering aftershave;
■ brown shoes with any colour suit except dark brown;
■ always wear a black belt unless you are wearing a brown suit;
■ white socks with any outfit!! (This is a golden rule for life: unless you are taking part in sport, there is no room in life for white socks.)
■ sandals or any type of open-toed shoe.

These all just go to prove that you do not really care about the job and all you are worried is about your own personal attitude, which may not be a great advertisement to someone who is looking for a colleague who is going to fit in. Once you've got the job there will be plenty of time to assess the 'real' dress code of the organisation.

Now what is it that you must wear? Colours that are suitable are the traditional blue and grey. Blacks and dark browns are fine as well, but are less conservative than blue and grey.

Whatever the role is, remember organisations do want disciplined, professional, responsible people in their jobs and it is best that you reflect that in your attire and attitude. White shirts, plain, striped or small patterned tie and jacket are *de rigueur* for guys, while for ladies, it's best to stick to a business suit if you can or alternatively a demure jacket/skirt/trousers combination work best.

In all cases, never wear brand new clothes. You don't want to be sitting down to the embarrassing sound of a too-tight seam on your trousers parting company or be near to tears because those new shoes really are a tight fit!

I know, I know, it sounds like advice from two centuries ago, but believe me, most interviewers are conservative in outlook and do actually believe this stuff. As they are the ones with all the power and you are playing in their back garden, you need to adapt YOU to fit them, not the other way around.

If you are still unsure , it does make sense to call and ask beforehand what the dress code is and then dress appropriately.

You are trying to make the interview as memorable for good reasons as you can, so to that end:
- **Do not** eat garlic for 48 hours before the interview.
- **Do not** smoke for an hour before hand. If you do, make sure you are able to wash your hands and freshen your breath before you go in.
- **Do not** ever, ever, EVER chew gum!

WHAT SHOULD I TAKE WITH ME?

The answer to this will depend on the role and perhaps whether or not you will be required to do a presentation. I will cover presentations in the next section.

It is a good idea to take a copy of your CV with you for your own reference. I have seen many candidates fumble and splutter when asked to talk through the CV simply through the pressure of the occasion. Unfortunately, a candidate who simply waffles or prevaricates at this time often comes across as 'shifty' or suspect. By having a copy to hand, you can glance at it and you will be surprised just how effective a prompt a peripheral glimpse of a past employer's name or an old job title is!

Do you have any, easy-to-read documentation that backs up your claims of success in the past? For example, you may wish to take copies of annual appraisals which show you in a good light. As these tend to be lengthy documents, highlight the narrative comments of your line and functional manager for the interviewer. If time allows they will read these, as they are much more insightful than formal references as many employers these days only supply basic, factual information on an employee's time with them for fear of litigation.

If you can, take hard-copy examples of work that you have done – particularly if it is new or innovative. Do not, under any circumstances, plagiarise anyone else's work! Also have consideration for copyright issues and do not take controlled documents with you without the appropriate permissions.

Again, time is the likely deciding factor for whether or not the interviewers will look at these. Often, it may even be the interviewers' curiosity that prompts them to ask what it is you have brought with you. It is a good idea to place anything you have brought to the interview in plain sight and to one side of the desk or table you are sitting at. If the interviewers have set the room up in a more casual manner, e.g. with their chairs at 45 degrees to you, then place it at your feet on the side that faces them. If possible utilise clear-covered folders rather than have them within a posh leather folio.

It is a good idea to take a notepad and pen with you too. At the outset of the interview ask if it is all right for you to take notes during the employer's input as you may wish to ask questions based on what they say.

OUTSIDE THE DRAGON'S DEN

When you are shown to the waiting area, be polite and thank your guide. Once there, use your eyes and ears. Tannoy announcements may just give you some snippet of information that you did not know. Look at the walls. Are there copies of the Mission Statement? Are there copies of Quality Assurance awards? Are there pictures of past successes? There will most likely be trade magazines on a table for guests to peruse. If you are there in good time you will have the opportunity to scan these searching for any specific references to the organisation and also any other snippets which may be of use to you once your inside. All of these sources can yield little bits of data that can enhance your knowledge of the organisation and may inform your conversation once you are inside.

Sit up straight on the seats provided. I know, I'm being your mum again! The reason all this sounds so familiar is because it is a universal truth. When you are collected to go in, if you are sprawled all over their plush leather couches then the very first image of you (and there are varying reports of people making their mind up about someone within the first 10, 20, 30 seconds) will not be a complimentary one. Think of the interview process as having started the minute you enter the building. Be polite to every member of staff whom you encounter. Your big chance starts here!

CHAPTER 3

LEGISLATION THAT EMPLOYERS NEED TO COMPLY WITH

While it is not the purpose of this text to be a reference book on employment law, I have included this chapter to make you aware of the legislative aspect of recruitment. Employers have to ensure they comply with the varying pieces of law and regulations or suffer not only punitive fines but also immeasurable damage to their reputation as an employer. Discrimination claims of all types are heard in the employment tribunals in Scotland, England and Wales. Employers may also be liable to make compensatory awards to those whom they have wronged. If you have a basic awareness of what an employer can and cannot do in the interview situation, then you are more likely to know whether or not you have the right to seek remedy at tribunal.

At the end of the chapter, I will briefly discuss employment tribunals should you decide to make a claim if you believe you have been unlawfully discriminated against when you have applied for a job and failed to be appointed. *Note*: This legislation applies in the United Kingdom only.

LEGISLATION AFFECTING RECRUITMENT

Employers have a legal responsibility to ensure no unlawful discrimination occurs in the recruitment and selection process on the grounds of sex, race, disability, age, sexual orientation and religion or belief. The following acts set out the legal requirements and areas they cannot discriminate in and are further discussed below:

- Rehabilitation of Offenders Act 1974
- Sexual Discrimination Act 1975
- Race Relations Act 1976
- Trade Union and Labour Relations (Consolidation) Act 1992
- Disability Discrimination Act 1995
- Asylum and Immigration Act 1996
- Police Act 1997
- Data Protection Act 1998
- Employment Equality Regulations 2003.

REHABILITATION OF OFFENDERS ACT 1974

This act deals with spent criminal convictions.

SEX DISCRIMINATION ACT 1975

This Act is concerned with discrimination on the grounds of sex. gender reassignment or marital status, either directly or indirectly, and covers a broad range of workers including contract workers and applies regardless of length of service in employment or the numbers of hours worked. It allows you to take a case to an employment tribunal. If your case is successful, you will receive compensation for any financial loss you have suffered; an award for injury to feelings can also be made.

The types of unlawful discrimination under the Sex Discrimination Act are:

- **Direct sex discrimination** is less favourable treatment of a woman than a man (or vice versa) because of her sex, for example refusing to consider women for a mechanic's job because of her sex, or for refusing to consider a man for a nursery nurse's job.
- **Direct marriage discrimination** is less favourable treatment of a married person compared to a single person of the same sex, for example having a policy of not employing married women.

- **Indirect sex discrimination** occurs when an employer applies a provision, criterion or practice equally to both women and men but which puts or would put women at a particular disadvantage when compared to men (or vice versa) and which the employer cannot show to be a proportionate means of achieving a legitimate aim. An example of this might be where an employer applies a provision that all job applicants must have been previously employed by the Armed Forces; as women have not traditionally worked in the Armed Forces in the same numbers as men, fewer women than men would be eligible to apply and so women would be put at a disadvantage.
- **Indirect marriage discrimination** occurs when an employer applies a provision, criterion or practice equally to both married women and single women (or married men and single men) but which puts or would put married persons at a particular disadvantage when compared to single persons of the same sex and which the employer cannot show to be a proportionate means of achieving a legitimate aim. An example of this might be a provision that applicants for promotion must be prepared to relocate to a different part of the country. As fewer married women than single women are mobile (and also, arguably, fewer married men than single men), this may be unlawful indirect marriage discrimination, unless the employer could show that mobility was a valid and necessary function of the job and was thus a proportionate means of achieving a legitimate aim.

Be aware however, that in certain limited circumstances it is lawful to discriminate in recruitment, training, promotion and transfer in a job for which the sex of the worker is a genuine occupational qualification (GOQ). The SDA allows an employer to restrict applications for a vacancy to women (or men) if the essential nature of the job, or particular duties attached to the job, calls for a woman (or a man).

GOQs can only be claimed in relation to:

- physiology (excluding physical strength and stamina) – for example, a female model for women's clothes;
- privacy and decency – for example, a male care assistant whose job involves helping men dress or use the toilet;
- certain work in private homes – for example, a live-in carer;
- single-sex accommodation – for example, working on board a submarine;
- single-sex establishments – can only be claimed when the jobholder has to live in the premises provided, which are normally occupied by persons of one sex and there is no separate sleeping accommodation for persons of the opposite sex;
- personal welfare or educational services – for example, a female counsellor in a rape crisis centre;
- jobs outside the UK in a country whose laws or customs are such that the job can only effectively be done by a man;
- the employment of married couples – for example, residential posts of female warden and male caretaker.

An employer cannot claim that a GOQ applies if there are enough other members of staff of the appropriate sex to cover the duties in question. For example, it would be unlawful for an employer to restrict a vacancy in a clothes shop to women on the grounds that part of the duties involved assisting in the changing room if there were enough women sales assistants already employed to cover that aspect of the job.

But how can I find out if I was rejected for a post because of my sex?

In order to successfully make a claim of direct sex discrimination, you have to show that you would have been appointed if not for your sex. You can do this by showing that you were better qualified and experienced than the successful candidate. You may know little about the employer and his recruitment practices; you may not know anything about the successful candidate. In these circumstances, it is important to use the Sex Discrimination Questionnaire (SD74) which can be obtained from the Equal Opportunities Commission's website at www.eoc.org.uk. The form gives you the opportunity to ask the employer particular questions which will help you find out more information. You can ask the employer questions about the successful candidate, including details of their sex, skills, qualifications and experience. You can also ask for details of the recruitment process, including how many men and how many women applied, the sex of all those interviewed, their qualifications and experience. This information should help you find out whether you have sufficient grounds for proceeding with a sex discrimination claim. For example, suppose you were not shortlisted, but you find out that all of the shortlisted candidates were better qualified than you and that both men and women were shortlisted – this would tell you that there would be little point in pursuing a case of sex discrimination.

RACE RELATIONS ACT 1976

The employer is prevented from treating an individual in a less favourable way because of their race or ethnic background.

This can be via direct discrimination which is where an employer discriminates directly against a certain group or individual because of their sex, race, disability, age, sexual orientation or religion or belief. For example, an employer may not want to employ women within the work place or individuals from a certain race. However, the law does not take into account that the employer may have chosen to discriminate against someone for their own protection – for example, the decision not to employ a black person may have been to protect the individual from racist comments.

Alternatively it can come from indirect discrimination which is where an employer discriminates against a group or individual without perhaps realising they have done so.

TRADE UNION AND LABOUR RELATIONS (CONSOLIDATION) ACT 1992

This Act applies to discrimination on the basis of whether or not an applicant is a trade union member.

DISABILITY DISCRIMINATION ACT 1995

The DDA places obligations on employers not to discriminate against disabled people either indirectly or directly. It also places an additional duty on employers to make 'reasonable adjustments' to accommodate a disabled person's needs should they be suitable for a position and would have been selected were it not for their disability.

Direct discrimination

Determination of whether there has been discrimination under the DDA usually involves comparing – asking 'how would the employer's treatment of me have been different if I was somebody else?' The 'somebody else' is known as a comparator. It can be a real person or a hypothetical person. The comparator can be a person without a disability, or a person not having the same disability as the disabled person making the claim (that is, you). You will see how this might work below.

Direct discrimination happens when an employer's treatment of the disabled person is because of that person's disability and the employer treats the disabled person less well than they would treat a comparator – that is, a non-disabled person or a person not having that particular disability (you will hear this called 'less favourable treatment') AND the relevant circumstances – and abilities – of the comparator are pretty much the same (in ways that count) as those of the disabled person. This part of the DDA became law in October 2004. However, employment tribunals have not decided many cases about this kind of comparing as we have gone to press.

Failure to make reasonable adjustments

This happens when an employer (or potential employer) has failed to make adjustments which are reasonable to accommodate the person's disability to the physical working environment (for example, things such as doorways, toilets, office furniture, etc.) where this failure places a disabled person at a substantial disadvantage and/or the employer's criteria or practices (for example, their selection and interview procedures, the terms on which employment is offered and conditions of service) place the disabled person at a substantial disadvantage and/or where the employer has failed to make an adjustment which they had already accepted was reasonable and where the employer knew or could reasonably be expected to know that the person concerned had a disability.

If the employer does not make reasonable adjustments then you may have a claim that unlawful discrimination has happened. If you can show that the employer has failed to make an adjustment, the employer cannot defend this failure. Examples of reasonable adjustments are given below.

You would need to:

- identify whether it is a physical feature of the building where you work which puts you at a substantial disadvantage;
- identify whether it is a 'provision, criterion or practice' which places you at a disadvantage;
- identify what the substantial disadvantage is and how it affects you;
- have made the employer aware that you are a disabled person and that you require appropriate reasonable adjustments.

The duty to make reasonable adjustments is owed specifically to the individual disabled person (that is, you). It does not matter that a non-disabled person (or a person not having your particular disability) would not have been put at a substantial disadvantage because of the employer's 'provisions, criteria or practices' or by a physical feature of the premises. What counts is that you (the disabled person) are at a disadvantage.

What is reasonable?

If the adjustment you require is a reasonable one then the employer must make it. However, an employer may say that the adjustment you require is not 'reasonable' in the circumstances. For example because:

- the cost of the adjustment is too great;
- the adjustment is not practical;
- the adjustment would cause too much disruption;
- the adjustment would not have the desired effect.

It would be for an employment tribunal to decide whether the employer's reasons adequately explain why the adjustment was not reasonable and was not made.

Examples of reasonable adjustments

Reasonable adjustments that an employer (or potential employer) should consider making include:

- allocating some of the disabled person's duties to another person;
- altering the disabled person's working hours or training;
- transferring the disabled person to a different place of work or training;
- giving or arranging for training or mentoring;
- allowing the person to be absent during working or training hours for rehabilitation, assessment or treatment;
- acquiring or modifying equipment (for example, providing voice-activated computer software for an employee with a visual impairment);
- modifying or adjusting disciplinary and grievance procedures;

- adjusting redundancy selection criteria;
- altering physical features of the building/office layout.

Disability-related discrimination

Disability-related discrimination happens when an employer's treatment of the disabled person is for a reason related to their disability and is less favourable than the way in which others, to whom that disability-related reason does not apply, are or would be treated and which the employer is unable to justify and/or when the employer has failed to make a reasonable adjustment, which would have made a difference to the reason the employer has given justifying its less favourable treatment.

To work out if disability-related discrimination has happened to you, you need to identify whether a disability-related reason is a factor in the treatment you are receiving and identify in what way the treatment that you are receiving is less favourable compared to others to whom the disability-related reason does not apply, and consider whether the explanation for the treatment, if any, put forward by the employer could justify the discrimination. This means that you would have to look at whether there is a strong link between the explanation given for your treatment and your circumstances. You would also have to consider whether the explanation carried real weight. You would also need to consider whether the employer had failed to make a reasonable adjustment and, if so, whether, had an adjustment been made, it would have made a difference to the explanation that the employer used to justify the less favourable treatment.

ASYLUM AND IMMIGRATION ACT 1996

The Asylum and Immigration Act makes it a criminal offence for an employer to employ those who do not have permission to work in the UK. Be aware, then, that the employer is likely to ask you to provide one of the following:

1. A passport showing that the applicant is a British citizen or has the right to abode in the UK.
2. A document showing that the applicant is a national of a European Economic Area country or Switzerland. This must be a national passport or national identity card.
3. A residence permit issued by the Home Office which has an endorsement stating that the applicant has a current right to residence in the UK as the family member of a national from a European Economic Area country or Switzerland.
4. A passport or other travel document endorsed to show that the applicant can stay indefinitely in the UK or has no time limit on his or her stay.
5. A passport or other travel document endorsed to show that the applicant can stay in the UK and that this endorsement allows the applicant to do the type of work the employer is offering if he or she does not have a work permit.
6. An Application Registration Card issued by the Home Office to an asylum seeker stating that the applicant is permitted to take employment.

Alternatively, the applicant can provide two of the following original documents:

First combination:

- A document giving the person's permanent National Insurance Number and name. This could be a P45, P60, National Insurance Card or a letter from a government agency. Along with checking and copying a document giving the person's National Insurance Number, the employers must also check and copy only one of the following documents:
- A full birth certificate issued in the UK, which includes the names of the applicant's parents; OR
- A birth certificate issued in the Channel Islands, the Isle of Man or Ireland; OR

- A certificate of registration or naturalisation stating that the applicant is a British citizen; OR
- A letter issued by the Home Office which indicates that the person named in it can stay indefinitely in the UK or has no time limit on his or her stay; OR
- An Immigration Status Document issued by the Home Office with an endorsement indicating that the person named in it can stay indefinitely in the UK or has no time limit on his or her stay; OR
- A letter issued by the Home Office which indicates that the person named in it can stay in the UK and this allows him or her to do the type of work the employer is offering; OR
- An Immigration Status Document issued by the Home Office with an endorsement indicating that the person named in it can stay in the UK and this allows him or her to do the type of work that is being offered.

Second combination:

- A work permit or other approval to take employment that has been issued by Work Permits UK. Along with a document issued by Work Permits UK, the employer should also see, check and copy one of the following documents:
- A passport or other travel document endorsed to show that the holder is able to stay in the UK and can take the work permit employment in question; OR
- A letter issued by the Home Office confirming that the person named in it is able to stay in the UK and can take the work permit employment in question.

POLICE ACT 1997

The Police Act provides a statutory basis for certain criminal record checks which may be used by employers. These checks can be made via the Criminal Records Bureau which came into being in 2001.

Organisations who work with vulnerable children or adults tend to utilise this service.

EMPLOYMENT EQUALITY REGULATIONS 2003

These regulations relate to sexual orientation, religion or belief and age.

Equality of opportunity should be an integral part of the recruitment and selection process. Employers may be required to offer training and assistance to under-represented groups. For example:

- pre-application assistance to applicants without English as their first language.;
- adverts to include a statement encouraging applications from under-represented groups.

DATA PROTECTION ACT 1998

Recruitment involves the gathering of personal information on candidates. Recruiting managers must therefore ensure that they comply with the requirements of the Data Protection Act in the way they obtain and handle this information.

THE EMPLOYMENT TRIBUNAL

A tribunal is less formal than a magistrate's court or county court but, like a court, it has procedures and rules. There is a panel of three members. The chairman is a lawyer. One of the other two members is from an employer panel, the other from an employee panel.

When you take a discrimination claim it is up to you to convince the tribunal that you have been discriminated against. The person you say discriminated against you will defend the claim and try to persuade the tribunal that you have not been discriminated against. Throughout the process you are known as the claimant and your opponent as the respondent. Together you are known as the parties to a claim.

You can bring claims against individual employees who you believe have discriminated against you as well as the employer. It is important to name individual employees as respondents as well as the employer if there is any possibility that the employer might be able to persuade the tribunal that it took reasonable steps to prevent the discrimination you are complaining about.

To help you decide whether or not to take a claim to the tribunal, it is worth considering what you hope to achieve and whether this is something the tribunal can order if your claim succeeds. A tribunal can:

- make a decision on whether or not the law has been broken;
- award compensation for your financial loss because of the treatment.;
- award compensation for injury to feelings suffered as a result of the treatment;
- award compensation for injury to health suffered as a result of the treatment;
- in certain circumstances order exemplary damages to punish the respondent;
- award interest on compensation.

Like all legal environments, there are certain burdens of proof before a claim can be successful and a number of decisions regarding the shift in the burden of proof in discrimination cases have been heard in the Court of Appeal. The court states that, when considering discrimination cases, a tribunal has to conduct a two-stage exercise.

First the claimant has to prove discrimination (i.e. facts from which the tribunal could conclude that, in the absence of an adequate explanation, the respondent has committed an unlawful act of discrimination); then the respondent had to prove they did not commit the unlawful act.

The decision makes it clear that to succeed in relation to the first stage of the test, a claimant must prove on the balance of probabilities facts which, in the absence of an adequate explanation, would be discrimination.

In assessing the first stage, the court states that it is important to bear in mind that it is unusual to find direct evidence of discrimination. It is also important to consider what inferences could be drawn from the facts. For example, inferences could be drawn from an evasive or equivocal reply to a race relations or sex discrimination questionnaire, or a failure to comply with a relevant code of practice.

Once a claimant had passed this first stage of the test, the tribunal should then go on to consider the second stage.

This stage, i.e. once the burden of proof has shifted to the respondent, involves the respondent proving on the balance of probabilities that the treatment was in no way whatsoever on the ground of sex or race or disability. Therefore it is not enough for the respondent to provide an explanation for the facts; they must show that sex, race or disability were not grounds for the treatment in question.

As you can see, the law is very complex in this area and I would urge you at this point to consider taking professional advice should you feel that the prospective employer has treated you in a way which contravenes any of the Acts mentioned above.

CHAPTER 4

UNDERSTANDING THE EMPLOYERS' PERSPECTIVE

Knowing what employers will be doing and thinking will give you an insight into their processes and thoughts. This will help you better prepare for your interview.

PREPARATION

In order to get the best out of any interview, employers should have prepared thoroughly. Once they have shortlisted candiates and decided on the interview date, they should have tried to find a good location - a quiet office or room which is free from interruptions and suitable for all candidates. They should have considered whether any of the candidates attending are disabled, as it may be necessary to consider whether any adjustments to the process need to be made, such as holding the interview in a brightly lit or wheelchair accessible room. Hopefully they will use a room that will creates a good impression!

Good practice states that two managers and an HR representative are present at interviews to minimise any bias and provide protection against any discrimination claims that the candidate could make from a one-to-one interview. Obviously the size and the resources of the organisation will have a bearing on who actually interviews.

Be aware that when employers use two or more interviewers, they may have agreed in advance who should ask which questions. This may mean your head turns from interviewer to interviewer like watching a tennis match!

When selecting interview questions, the interviewers should have made themselves familiar with the application forms or CVs, job description and person specification. To avoid discrimination and to assist the interviewers in making an informed and fair decision, they are highly likely to be asking the same questions of each candidate; however, individualised questions may be needed during the interview to follow up on particular answers or circumstances. This is perfectly acceptable as long as the questions relate to the your suitability for the job and do not stray into irrelevant personal details.

Most questions used should be based on the Job Description and Person Specification which they initially based their shortlist on, so make sure you have a good grasp of the detail contained within each of these documents (if supplied to you) so that you may tailor your answers appropriately.

In order to encourage individuals to talk, interviewers often use open questions which cannot be answered with 'yes' or 'no' and often begin with 'what', 'why', 'how' or 'when'. So be prepared to do the lion's share of the talking! Incidentally, good interviewing practice has it that candidates do 80 per cent of the talking and the interviewers only 20 per cent.

CONDUCTING THE INTERVIEW

A good interviewer will explain the structure of the interview - i.e. provide you with some background information, tell you that they will be asking a series of questions and allow some time at the end to discuss any questions that you may have – and how long it will last.

During the course of the interview the interviewers may fall silent. Remember, the aim of the interview is to gain as much information as possible from you to establish if you are suitable for the job. They should know that any silences caused by you could just be that you are considering your question. Don't, however, be afraid to use terms such

'Hmm, let me think about that for a moment' to make sure they are aware that you haven't just gone blank.

They will probably take notes throughout the interview, so don't be put off by the lack of eye contact.

At the end of the interview, the interviewer may make sure that you are familiar with the terms and conditions of the job and that they are acceptable. You should be informed what will happen next and when a decision will be made. If not, ask!

Since a contract of employment can be formed by a verbal offer and acceptance, interviewers should ensure that they do not use words that could be construed as an offer unless this is what they intend. In most cases – and particularly where the job offer is to be made is subject to conditions such as satisfactory references – it is likely that your interviewer will say at best that they will recommend that an offer be made or that an offer will be sent out in due course. The most common approach is to make the offer afterwards. Interviewers will be aware that promises made to successful candidates at their interview can end up as part of their contract of employment, so are likely to be cagey in going into too much detail about what any offer would entail. Remember, statements made at interview can also be used as evidence of the terms of the contract if there is subsequently a dispute about its content.

THE IMPORTANCE OF INTERVIEW NOTES

Taking notes throughout the interview is important because it not only assists recruiters in their decision-making and helps when providing candidate feedback but it also helps should their decision ever be seen as 'unfair' by an unsuccessful candidate.

The Data Protection Act 1998 enables candidates to see interview notes when they form a set of information on that candidate. It is your right to ask to see these notes at any time (subject to the payment of an administration fee in some cases).

CHAPTER 5

CONDUCTING YOURSELF AT THE INTERVIEW

There is a variety of different types of interview: such as one-to-one, panel and group interviews. The style of the interviewers will vary too – some will seem very stern and assertive while others will be more welcoming and engaging. In every case though, there are basic principles that you should adopt in how you deport yourself and behave during the interview.

I make no apologies for using the word 'behave' as there used to be a (now discredited) style of interview where the interviewers were deliberately antagonistic, the idea being to see if they could get the poor candidate to behave as they would when working under pressure. Thankfully, this practice is very rare these days and you are unlikely to have to suffer the torment of this.

OK, basic principles then –

- When you first enter the room make sure you have good posture and make eye contact with everyone in the room.
- As you are introduced to everyone, give a firm (not too firm) handshake. If you are prone to sweaty palms, make sure you discreetly wipe them before you commence shaking hands.
- Scan the room layout once only and maintain eye contact with the lead or only interviewer.
- Look alert and wait to be asked to sit down.
- If you are offered a tea or coffee, politely decline. Its only another thing that can go wrong – like spilling it down yourself or worse still knocking it over!

- Three rules of behaviour in the interview are professionalism professionalism, and professionalism! That's not to say you can't use humour where appropriate, but remember, it's not a comedy audition and stay well away from areas of humour that could remotely be considered offensive.
- You are likely to be asked if you found your way to the interview venue easily. Always answer positively, even if it was a nightmare getting there. These people will be so used to getting to those premises that it will jar in their minds if you moan about not being able to find the building. You are trying to build a consistently positive picture in your mind from the word 'go'.
- If you are asked about your well-being generally, e.g. 'So how are you today then Ellie?' never, ever answer in the negative! Not even slightly negative such as 'Oh, you know' or 'So-so'. Be positive and enthusiastic – 'Very well thank you. And you?' This is common social interaction that oils the wheels a little. Be polite. End of lecture.

Ok, so the interview is under way. You may be asked to talk through your career to date. This is where your copy of your CV comes in handy to have in front of you. As I said in Chapter 2, it's amazing what a visual prompt can do for the memory. When talking about your career to date, don't repeat merely what it says on your CV. Your interviewers will have read it already and are looking for you to expand on what it contains. If you've done your own competency profiling as I suggested in Chapter 2, you will be able to talk about your various positions in terms of your competencies and, more importantly, achievements. Always accentuate anything of note that you were responsible for. Beware, however, of over-exaggerating your role in the success of an organisation. In a recent reality TV show that sought a budding entrepreneur to work with a highly successful and well-known London-based businessman, a contestant claimed that through her efforts her company increased its turnover by several million pounds. 'What? By yourself?' asked the stony-faced interviewer. The resultant spluttering of the contestant was a joy to behold – if you are prone to Schadenfreude that is! If you were part of a team that achieved noticeable results, be honest. Don't try to hog all the glory for yourself.

In terms of the body language you should exhibit throughout the interview, I would say don't sit to rigidly upright in your chair but don't slouch either. For those of you who have dabbled or been involved in training in neurolinguistic programming (NLP)[1] do not on any account fall into the trap of 'mirroring' the interviewer closely in order to build rapport. Guess what? We've heard of it, and unless you are a master at it, it will come over as false and manipulative. I've personally experienced it once and clocked it after a few minutes. I had quite a bit of fun moving my hair about and varying which leg I crossed etc. I almost forgot about the questions I was asking this guy, such was the fun I was having.

Its easy to say 'be yourself', but really that's exactly what you should be. The interactions between you and the interviewer (who may well turn out to be your new boss) will then be genuine and honest, and a good guide to whether or not you are going to get on.

The following chapters are about giving you the ammunition to come back with well-thought out answers to tough questions.

Note
1. In NLP, practitioners are advised to match, as if in a mirror, the gestures, postures and even breathing rates of the person they are attempting to establish rapport with. NLP holds that subconscious signals are sent to the other person which guides them into thinking favourably of you.

CHAPTER 6

COMMON INTERVIEW QUESTIONS ... AND HOW TO ANSWER THEM

QUESTIONS ABOUT YOUR DRIVE FOR ACHIEVEMENT

Q Tell me what you know about our business?

This question falls into this category as the new employer will be assuming that you want to join their firm because it is a sound and progressive career move for you. It is, isn't it? That's a hint ... Again, this question will come up time after time. You expected it to be asked. Didn't you? So you went onto the Internet and 'Googled' their name. You went onto the corporate website and noted down some facts and figures.

> *Well, you employ some 15,000 people in over 12 countries, your main areas of operation are in textiles and in paper, your ...*

Zzzzzzz – I'm asleep already. Any fool can regurgitate facts from a website. It doesn't mean you know anything about the company at all. Now while I'm not suggesting that you don't quote them some devastatingly interesting statistics around their niche market specialisms etc., what I am saying is get behind the facts that they present to you. What is their market share? Who are their competitors? What threats are there to their continuing growth? What opportunities might they wish to exploit? What did their CEO say in their last annual report?

By all means use the net, but don't just settle for the party line. Find out who their competitors are and what they are saying. Find out the registered office of the company and telephone their marketing department and request that they send out to you a copy of the most recent annual report. By law in the UK, PLCs must comply with this request from any person. I have had some fun over the years reminding junior clerks of this!

Can you imagine interviewing five people and all of them trot out the same facts and figures taken from the same source? What if the sixth interviewee reminds you that at the moment you are only number two in the world market; however, the CEO has a strategy in place to take you to number one, and that involves ... No contest! Get him/her back for a final interview!

I'm asking you to be a bit smarter than the average bear on this one. Be creative about how you illustrate what you know about their company.

Q Give an example of when you've experienced a setback

If you are asked this question at interview and you are unprepared for it you will probably make a hash of it. No question. It's the interviewer mining that negativity seam again and your auto-response will be to go into denial about it. After all, someone as brilliant as me gets it right first time, every time, don't I?

The trick here is to recall a time when, although the eventual outcome was positive, the success was down to either your intervention or your realisation that what you were doing first time round was not working. There's no shame in admitting that your initial approach to a situation turned out to be less effective than you'd hoped, but through your well developed sense of self-awareness, you changed some or all aspects of your approach and achieved the aim after all.

Interviewers will be expecting you to describe the situation, your thinking behind why you initially did what you did, how you reacted to the realisation that it wasn't working and maybe the reaction of others round about you. For example:

We had a situation in my last place where team leaders were identified as needing training in the various areas of management expertise in order for them to perform at the level at which the company expected them to. My initial thought was to get them an off-the-shelf training course which would supply these skills. I booked them onto a course at the local college, which meant they would attend on a half-day release basis on various days of the week. I informed their managers of what I had done, emphasising how I had arranged it so that not all the team leaders would be away from work at the same time. A few weeks passed and although I was getting anecdotal evidence from the shop floor about the course, when I got the first report from the college which showed nearly half of the employees who were supposed to be attending only did so intermittently I was shocked. I immediately arranged for these guys to come in and see me on a one-to-one basis to find out why they hadn't been going. During these interviews I discovered that many of them were actually scared of the traditional classroom environment and for most of them, the last time they had been in that environment was when they were 16! It was obvious to me then that this methodology wasn't going to work for all of them, so I took a poll of all of the team leaders to identify who would rather not be in the classroom environment. Of the 26 team leaders seven said they were actively resistant to it and two were unsure. I then did some research and found that I could have these nine guys do an NVQ-based qualification with the learning provider actually coming on site to deliver the more formal parts in our own training room. The qualification that they would gain would be broadly similar to those attending the college course, so that was a bonus. I also successfully negotiated a partial refund from the college for the guys we took out as they hoped to get more business from us in the future In hindsight, perhaps I should have had more dialogue with those who were going to be affected by the training and sought to supply a training methodology to suit their needs.

This answer contains all the essential elements: an outline of the circumstances; your initial approach; your recognition that it wasn't working; your gathering of data to come up with an alternative solution; the implementation of that solution and its subsequent success; and finally a recognition of where you went wrong in the first place.

Q What have you done to progress your education to date?

Obviously I cannot state here what you should be saying in terms of formal education because you will all have different experiences. However, education comes in many forms – and you should talk with enthusiasm about this ...

Well, I left school with a few GCSEs and one A level and started in company ABC's sales department. The company sold house and car insurance via their call centres. After I had received my initial training for the job I was taken on for, there were a few opportunities for me to attend short training sessions such as assertiveness training and customer care etc. but I realised I was capable of a lot more so I asked my team leader if I could perhaps spend some time in other departments such as the underwriters room. They seemed to be pleased with my enthusiasm so they let me spend a month watching and learning what they did in that department. As a result, when a vacancy came up I was the obvious choice for the role and got a position in there. When I was there, I asked the company to support me in going to night school to gain insurance qualification, and I'm pleased to say that they did – as you can see from my application.

This answer conveys several attractive qualities from the employer's perspective: enthusiasm, loyalty, a willingness to broaden your skill base, a recognition of the importance of industry-specific formal qualifications and a desire to be proactive in your career.

QUESTIONS ABOUT YOUR STRATEGIC THINKING

You may think that this section is not really for you and be tempted to skip by it because you've never worked in a role where you've been expected to think 'strategically' – don't!! Strategy is not all about top-level corporate decision-making or 'blue-sky thinking' needing the mental capacity of Einstein. Its about thinking further ahead than the completion of the current task. I bet you do it all the time but just don't give it such a grand name as 'strategy'.

Once you've read some of my examples, have a think about times when you have looked further than the end of your nose. Maybe it was simply organising your diary or even playing the 'long game' in terms of office politics.

Q 'In what past situations have you shown most evidence of visionary/strategic thinking?'

This question is aimed directly at you to get you to describe an occasion where you thought about things from a wider perspective. The trick here is not to go into too much detail because that will ultimately bore your interviewers. They will not have the same terms of reference that you have and will not be able to know about the characters involved. Like all your answers in the interview, they should be concise but with sufficient detail to get the highlights across. A typical answer would be:

In my department we basically processed papers that came from another department. Once we had done our bit, the papers went to a third department for them to work on. It meant that each of the three departments was only aware of their bit of the puzzle. Looking at each piece of the process like that was just the way things had always been done. In reality what it meant was that there was lots and lots of communication via e-mails and telephone conversations throughout the day where people were seeking confirmation of something being done or clarification on a point, etc. We were even on different floors in the building, so nipping into the next office wasn't on either. I took a proposal to my boss outlining my plans for multidisciplinary teams, teams made up of representatives of all three departments. My rationale was that we could each have a client base or set of key accounts so that between us we would handle all their needs from enquiry to dispatch. It also meant that the client could have a single point of contact with our firm for all their enquiries, no matter what the subject was. I explained to my boss that there would be training needs for us all where we would all need to acquire the skills necessary to do two jobs previously done by others. It would also mean some office moving and equipping, because I thought that we'd need new, round tables, so each team could work facing each other making it easier for information to flow round the team. We had had a problem with people leaving before due to the repetitive nature of the work, and I was sure that this new way of working would help counter that due to the increase in variety for the individual. The customer would receive a slicker operation too. I'm pleased to say that we trialled it in our branch and it worked so well that we rolled it out throughout the country. My boss complimented me on 'seeing the bigger picture' and made mention of it during my appraisal.

This answer not only shows a continuous improvement attitude, but that you were able to demonstrate an ability to think of the wider implications for the organisation, not just the team you were working in.

Q What do you see as the main threats to our business in the long term? What can we do to ensure long-term success?

As I have said earlier in this book, most employers will expect you to have researched them to some extent on the Internet or in the library. This approach will give you lots of statistics and facts about them – **ones that they wish you to know.** What a company's website will not give you is information on their competitors or the state of the market that they are in, or developments that their competitors have that may influence their position in the marketplace. My advice to you then is that when you do your research, find out who their direct competitors are and go to their websites too. Try to get a global viewpoint of their market as a whole. Ask yourself what external influences there are on their products or services – for example, changes in legislation such as the introduction of smoke-free workplaces may have a negative effect on those organisations that make products related to smoking – tobacco, paper, filters, etc. – but may have a positive effect on those organisations providing employers with 'no smoking' signs or who manufacture smoking shelters etc. A typical answer would be:

As your organisation manufactures bread and bakery products, I believe that it may be subject to external influences such as the price of grain because poor harvests in grain-producing countries can have a dramatic effect on your raw material costs. I'm sure the Atkins Diet craze had a negative effect too through people consuming less carbohydrates, but I think these effects are more likely to be short lived. I'd bet that if we had a long, dry summer, more people would be having barbecues, and as hamburgers are very popular for barbecues, then people will need more bread rolls to put them in. During my research on your company and its competitors [it's great if you can actually TELL them you've done research] I see that XYZ Bakeries and Ubiquitous Bakeries have both opened new plants in this part of the country. This would tell me that this is still a growing market for them to invest in new plant and they might see benefits from economies of scale as they get larger which would drive their costs down, making them more profitable and therefore more competitive. I also saw that XYZ have developed a new process which reduces the baking time of a loaf by 20 per cent. This will also make them tough to compete against.

I would say in order to secure the long-term success of your business you will need to ensure that you are keeping up with technological advances in the manufacture of your product, you will have to tie your suppliers down to deals which secure your supply of raw material with minimal fluctuations in price and you will need to ensure that your distribution system is at least as good as your competitors for you to keep abreast of them in terms of goods to market as fresh as is possible.

This answer demonstrates your commercial and business acumen by offering the employer a chance to see that you can develop an opinion based on various sources of information and not just regurgitate the corporate blurb.

QUESTIONS ABOUT YOUR RELATIONSHIP BUILDING

In the vast majority of working environments, people are required to interact with others on some level or other. Your potential new employer is looking to reassure themselves that you will 'fit in'. 'Is that strictly necessary?' I hear you ask in a fiendishly clever, Devil's advocate sort of way. Look at it this way: how do you feel about new people coming to spend time with you? Be truthful, would you more expect them to fit into you and your group's social 'norms', or feel that it's more you and your group's responsibility to fit in with the new person? Hmmm, call me psychic, but I'm betting it's the former.

The employer is using these questions in a two-pronged approach. Firstly, he or she may be exploring whether or not you can build relationships as that is part of the job requirement, or he/she might be seeking confirmation that you are of a similar personal disposition to the team where the vacancy lies.

My advice to you is, once again, to be true to yourself. If you try to adopt a persona that you feel is the type suited to the team in question and you get the job, it will not be that long before your true self comes out and that may be in conflict with others. There are not many people, actors excepted, that can carry off displaying behavioural characteristics that are different from their own for any length of time. You may also find that you have talked yourself into the job and regret it because your new colleagues 'are not your kind of people' either!

Q Tell me about a recent situation when you had to build a relationship with a new colleague. Why was the relationship important?

This question can be answered equally well from the point of view of a subordinate or a manager. As a manager your relationship with your direct reports will often influence how well your department performs, therefore it's imperative you get your team pulling *for you* as much as they are pulling for themselves. A typical answer might be:

When I took over as Team Leader in my last job, I realised that I'd have to gain credibility really quickly. I decided not to trot out the old platitudes about 'my door always being open' etc., but rather tried to make myself seem grounded and definitely on their side. I knew that one of the team had applied for my job and had the potential to undermine me from within, so one of my first tasks was to take him aside (I did 1-2-1 meetings with all of my staff in my first week) and shared with him my views on being new in the role. I told him I needed someone whom I could trust, to be my guide to office politics and to steer me through the minefield of the organisation's policies and procedures. He was delighted to be separated out from the rest of the team like that, to be treated like a trusted aide so quickly. However, I knew this was a high-risk strategy as he might have reacted negatively in a fit of pique, but thankfully it turned out well.

From a subordinate's position, a good answer might be:

When I first joined the team I realised that I had to fit in really quickly. I made sure I asked lots and lots of questions relating to my job, but I took an interest in people's personal lives too – without prying of course. I made sure that I remembered people's partner's names etc., and to ask how their children had got on at sports day, for example, if a colleague happened to mention she was excited about her son taking part. I was scrupulous in meeting deadlines or getting back to people when I said I would and I was always honest enough to admit when I didn't know something or couldn't help someone. That way people would trust me and I would be seen as credible and reliable.

Q Think of someone who's particularly effective at building and maintaining relationships with others. What do they do exactly?

This question is not only about you having self-awareness, but also the ability to spot such traits in others. You can use a bit of poetic licence here if you wish. After all, if you describe this person in the correct way, it could be Hamish McTavish from Glasgow (who might not even exist) to Sir Richard Branson (who may or may not be as you describe him). Either way, the crux of the matter here is for you to describe this person, ficticious or otherwise, using the right type of adjectives.

> I used to work with this chap called Ewan. I've never seen someone who could get so many people to do things for him when he needed them to or to be so readily accepted in any company. From my observations of him I saw that he always communicated in the same relaxed and friendly manner with everyone, no matter what their position in the company. He'd occasionally work late in order to get things completed for other people. He genuinely seemed to care about others and always made a point of being extra helpful to new people. I once asked him what he thought he did that made people trust him, and he simply told me that he always treated others like he expected to be treated: he was truthful, kept his promises, didn't make excessive demands on others, and acted on the basis that people are intrinsically good and would rather do you a good turn than a bad one. I suppose you might say that some could've thought him naïve, but I didn't. He lived up to his own ideals which made people round about him live up to them too.

Q How do you behave when you meet new people?

The reality might be that you might behave differently each time you meet new people. However, they really wouldn't ask you a question like this to get such a bland answer as that would they? No. If you didn't answer 'no' at this point, go stand in the corner and come and see me at home time.

What they are getting at here is – are you self-aware enough of your own behaviours and how they affect others? Can you adapt depending on the character or nature of who you are with?

I'm conscious that I don't dominate the conversation when I meet new people. I genuinely like people, so I ask a lot of questions – not enough to be accused of prying, but I always try and remember the details of what they say to me. Maybe it's their interests, or things they've said about their family. I then drop it into conversation and the response is usually positive.

QUESTIONS ABOUT YOUR COMMERCIAL AWARENESS

Your initial reaction to seeing a section devoted to commercial awareness might be 'Well, I don't really have to be that commercially aware do I? There are loads of people for that such as accountants, finance controllers etc.' The truth is, you really SHOULD have a commercial awareness no matter what line of business your employer is in. After all, if the enterprise is not successful, it won't be in existence for very long. Be aware that each and every employee, some way or another affects the bottom line of a business's balance sheet and you should be prepared to demonstrate how you contribute and your awareness of the 'bigger picture'. You may be looking to work for a non-profit-making organization. In this context, look at ways of minimising expenditure, which makes the money that does come in go that much farther.

Q Why, in your opinion, do customers choose our products and services?

The initial question here is almost designed for anyone who ever took a marketing course in the past or has a basic grasp of common sense (I know, I know, it's in short supply).

Well I think first and foremost your organisation has built up its brand to a point where people automatically think of you when they think of (their product/service here). My view is that people regard Company XYZ as one of the leaders in their field supplying this particular market in such a way that people know what to expect: a good product at a good price at the right time.

Q How could we make them more competitive?

'It is a basic fact of business that you can only make more profit by either (a) selling more product at the same margin, or (b) increasing

your margin, and you can only increase your margin by either raising selling prices or reducing selling costs. I don't really know enough about your particular business model to offer a serious opinion on what I think you should do. Do we have time to explore this further?'

Here again we have used honesty in admitting we don't have all the facts. The candidate who makes bold statements on how the people interviewing him have actually got it all wrong thus far is not brave, merely foolish! Again, you have shown good time awareness by asking if there is enough time to go deeper into this question.

Q What are the market trends that affect us?

Here is a chance for you to shine. You NEED to know the factors that affect your prospective employer's business.

For example, if they make items which are not considered to be good for us or the environment – cigarettes, sweets, 4 × 4 cars, nuclear reactors, etc. – then you should be aware of the mood of the country at that moment. Maybe there has been a lot of press coverage on childhood obesity and it's a boiled sweet manufacturer you are trying to work for. You might want to lead with

Has Company XYZ examined using sugar substitutes in its products?

I see the Chancellor has put the road tax levy up again for SUV vehicles. Is the industry lobbying Parliament to try and have this decision reversed? With the advent of biofuels, I'd have thought that the type of vehicles you make were ripe for this change in motoring.

There is no substitute for research here. Prospective employers will choose every single time someone who demonstrates a knowledge of their market over and above a candidate with specific knowledge of their business they've gleaned from the corporate website.

Q What opportunities have you had to identify cost savings in the past? Give an example.

Again, this is your most direct opportunity to demonstrate your contribution to the bottom line. If every employee came up with a single idea which saved the company money or increased its profitability, then that company would be successful beyond the dreams of avarice. It may seem like Utopia, but it's what employers want. Do yourself a favour and stand out from the herd by showing how you have been and will continue to be a positive item on the balance sheet!

In our department we kept a number of forms which employees needed to complete, such as a 'car registration form' which entitled them to a free parking pass on site, a 'holiday requisition form' and a 'bereavement leave application form', etc. This involved them leaving their place of work and calling in at our office. Employees always came during working hours, not break times. Sometimes they brought a mate with them to keep them company. I thought it was daft for them to come to us and the forms should be more local to them. My first thought was to supply all our team managers with paper copies so they would have their own supply, but then I remembered that we had a company-wide intranet site where forms could 'sit' and be downloaded only when needed. I had the IT people put them up on the site and then sent a global e-mail telling people about the changes. As a result, the traffic slowed to a trickle and lots of time was saved by people no longer coming over to our office.

Q How did you choose where to make the savings?

Our company was on the verge of going into austerity measures and we were all asked to think of ways to save money. We had lots of the usual ideas: using both sides of paper, trimming faxes so no blanks went through the machine, doing away with Post-it notes, etc. It just dawned on me that the biggest cost for us was people's time, so the more time we could save, the better. I then realised that it was actually other people's time in coming to see me and my colleagues that was the biggest waste, so I came up with the intranet idea.

When you come up with your own answer to this question, be sure to incorporate an element of you comparing options and going for the most practical/cost-effective/easily achieved, etc.

Q How much money do you think you saved?

At first we couldn't think how we were going to quantify the savings, but then we simply took an average number of calls a day we used to receive asking for forms, multiplied that by the average number of minutes the whole journey to and from our office took and then multiplied that by an average hourly rate figure given to us by finance. We reckoned on saving over £4,000 a year.

Never, ever, make wild claims on any savings you made – you might very well be asked to justify them.

QUESTIONS ABOUT YOUR LEADERSHIP OF CHANGE

More and more these days, the philosophy of 'continuous improvement' is being adopted and applied by organisations in every sector. By the very nature of continuous improvement, change is inevitable and indeed welcomed – but not by all. Some individuals react well to change and see this as a way of enriching or improving their working lives. Others are fearful of change and either resist overtly or by more subtle methods.

You may very well be asked about your experiences of change in the workplace and possibly how you have initiated or led change. This does not have to mean formal change programmes with milestones and Gantt charts and the like. It may mean simple changes to the way you have worked in the past that has accrued a benefit for the organisation. It may mean how you have reacted to a change thrust upon you. Either way, there is nothing as sure as change as organisations develop and evolve over time, so you should be equipped with the types of answers that employers want to hear.

Q **Tell us about a recent time when you had to adapt to a major change.**

■ **How did you adapt?**

■ **What was difficult about the transition?**

The clue to a good answer for this question is in the use of the word 'major'. Your interviewer is not looking for some answer in relation to how you changed suppliers for the photocopy paper for example. This is BIG change they are on about. Granted, you may not have been subject to big change, as not everybody has, so if you haven't, just say so.

I worked for an organisation which was a plc and the culture and style of how we worked was very much as you'd expect from a large organisation. We had the best equipment, flexible working practices, cheap gym membership, etc. However, the company's shares were bought by a group of venture capitalists and that's when the changes began. After a while, once the dust had settled, we started to get visits from people who were working on a 'synergy project'. We soon found out that this meant they were looking for ways to identify savings by seeing where we had functions and processes that could be carried out by the new owners' existing staff and they could cut costs by axing people and jobs at our end. After the HR function was moved to their head office along with finance and marketing, we realised that 'we weren't in Kansas any more' and that things were going to be a lot different. Where we always had a human being to talk to in relation to personnel matters, we now had to talk to a voice on the end of the phone and our calls were logged and we were given a 'case number'. Most people hated this and many complaints were lodged about it. I had heard of the 'Business Partner' approach to HR which has first-line managers carrying out many of the less complex functions of HR. I looked into this and suggested to my department head that all first-line managers get a grounding in discipline, grievance, recruitment and the like so that we could deal with our team members' basic stuff without them having to phone this hated 'hotline'. He put the idea up the chain of command and I'm pleased to say that we had a number of seminars on personnel subjects and we were given basic guide books to help us out. So what started off as a terrible situation turned out to be one where a lot of us were pleased to be receiving new and interesting training, and we provided a solution to the problem of there not being a human face there when people had problems.

Q **Tell us about a recent time when you questioned or challenged a way of working.**

- ■ **Why did you question it?**
- ■ **What alternative did you suggest?**
- ■ **To what extent were your ideas used?**

I worked in a factory where most of the jobs were not particularly complex, but nevertheless there were training periods required for someone to become competent in each of the roles they might be asked to fulfil. The system the company adopted was one where an inexperienced employee would work with someone who had more experience (although sometimes not a lot more) for around two weeks. The team leader would then go through a checklist and tick off all the various boxes which were supposed to indicate that the new person was competent in that role. I was asked to take part in what is known as an 'intervention'. This is where a focus group made up of employees from various departments around the factory would examine a particular issue and find ways to resolve whatever the perceived problem was. The problem we were looking at was the quality of training of new starts. During this intervention, I was given the task of reviewing these 'competency profiles' as the checklists were known. After a little while I noticed that the wording of these checklists was weighted towards what inputs the employee had been given. For example: 'Has the employee been shown where the red emergency stop button is located?' and 'Has the employee been told what is the correct personal protective equipment to wear?' What struck me was that someone could have been told vital information – such as how to halt the machine in an emergency – but there was no guarantee that they had absorbed this information and could put it into use! As a lot of the plant and equipment was potentially dangerous, I flagged this up to the intervention leader. I suggested that we change the wording on all the checklists to record that the individual has demonstrated their knowledge, not just record the fact that they'd been informed. For example: 'Can the employee demonstrate the location of and correct usage of the red emergency stop button?' and 'Can the employee demonstrate the correct personal protective equipment they must wear and how to use it?' I also flagged up the fact that we had team leaders who were signing off people as competent on a machine or process that they themselves had not been trained on.

After a discussion with the members of the intervention team, we made this one of our key recommendations of the project. As a result, each team leader was tasked with rewriting each of the competency profiles in use in their area and they also had to be signed off as competent on each machine or process that they were signing other people off on.

QUESTIONS ABOUT YOUR LEADERSHIP SKILLS

There comes a time in many people's career when they move up the greasy pole and take on the responsibility for others' work as well as their own. Many people only describe success in their chosen careers in terms of how far up the corporate tree they have climbed (to mix my metaphors). As yet, other methods of measuring career success have not fully been assimilated. So for the purposes of this chapter, we will treat any role that involves leading others as a 'good thing'. But have a look at what others have said about leadership before you decide exactly what type of a leader you are:

Dwight D. Eisenhower: 'You do not lead people by always hitting them over the head. That's assault, not leadership.'

Faye Wattleton: 'The only safe ship in a storm is leadership.' Who also said: 'Whoever is providing leadership needs to be as fresh and thoughtful and reflective as possible to make the very best fight.'

The former British Prime Minister, James Callaghan, said: 'A leader must have the courage to act against an expert's advice.' *A more recent British Prime Minister, Tony Blair, also famously said:* 'The art of leadership is saying no, not yes. Its very easy to say yes.'

The answers I have given below are written from the perspective of someone who has actually led others before. However, it is always going to be a difficult position for someone who has never been a leader before to get across how good they 'would be' as a leader, as they have not been tested. However, if you can grasp the underlying principles of the answers here, then you can adopt your response accordingly, to a '... well, if I had been in that situation, I would have ...' etc.

Q Describe a time when you had to coordinate the work of other people.

■ What were you trying to achieve?

■ How did you go about organizing the work?

This is the classic version of this question. This is the big pink neon sign that says: 'C'mon! Show us just what a brilliant leader you are!' You can adapt your answer to fit depending on whether or not you have experience in leadership.

I was working as a member of the production staff at XYZ Co. and this year they conducted an employee satisfaction survey. Once all the results were in, a focus group was formed to look at the results. I was nominated from our area to be part of this group. I thought at first it was just a matter of turning up and expressing my opinion about the results. I quickly found out that the company was deadly serious about making changes based on the results of this survey. One of the results that came out was that people often felt that they were kept in the dark about what was going on with the company. 'Mushroom management' was the way one person described it! An action was formulated that stated a sub-group would examine the options for improving communications on site and I was designated the 'action point owner.' I was given a free hand to choose three or four people from the entire workforce – both blue and white collar – to work on this with me. I had a timescale for feeding back recommendations to the focus group. I thought the best approach would be to have team members with different skill sets to help us achieve our goal which was effectively to provide the employees by suitable means with the type of information that they wanted to hear. I thought about the various elements of the action point and had an idea of who I wanted in the team. I convened a meeting quickly and designated each team member with a particular role. I had a secretary devise, distribute and collate the results of a simple questionnaire to determine what exactly people wanted to know about; I chose one chap from our buying department and he was tasked with finding out exactly what ways we could use to get our message across. That meant he was pricing up plasma TV screens, text-light boards, the cost of printing newsletters, etc. I chose one chap from our planning department who drew up a progress chart itemising all our actions and milestones. I chose one lady from production who I knew was a member of a writers circle. She would be tasked with producing the actual wording of anything we produced.

Over the course of the six-month project we met regularly to discuss our survey's findings, to come up with ideas for the media we would use to get the messages across, to iron out any difficulties we had and to discuss factual information such as the cost of buying and installing large-screen televisions etc.

My approach was that, like any good football team, you needed a mix of specialists. You couldn't win trophies with eleven strikers on the pitch. I was very fortunate in that we all worked well together. However, I am aware that sometimes there can be conflict in teams for any number of reasons, including personality clashes, but I did not have to cope with that. It was not all plain sailing of course as people had other commitments to attend to outside of working on this action. I had to learn diplomacy skills quite quickly to ensure that each team member contributed their bit on time and in full. As a result, we produced a set of recommendations, some of which were adopted without change and some were adopted in a less expensive form. In all I think I did well and received positive feedback from my manager, my team and the focus group.

Q Think of someone who is particularly effective in providing leadership. What do you think they do successfully?

Do you have a business hero? Honestly? I watched a certain BBC series recently. The premise was that 12 'candidates' lived together in a posh London house for 12 weeks and were split into two teams and had to take part in business simulations on a weekly basis, after which some poor sod from the losing team was 'fired'. This process went on until there was only one candidate left. The reward for the overall winner was a job with a well-known London-based businessman and a six-figure salary. Towards the end of this so-called 'job interview from hell', the business guru pulled in three of his closest advisers to conduct face-to-face interviews with the remaining five candidates. I hesitated to describe them as 'interviews'. Out and out maulings would be a better description! I'm happy to report, constant reader, that these were far removed from how 99.999999 per cent of employers, enlightened or otherwise, would behave during the interview. I digress. One of the interviewers asked one of the candidates why he wanted this particular job. 'Oh, Sir Albert Sweetner [name changed] is an all-time hero of mine. I was aware of him as a boy growing up and I've always wanted to work for him'. As you can imagine, the interviewer was close to throwing up (as was I watching this). When challenged on his strange taste in boyhood heroes, our extremely clever but demonstrably addled candidate continued along this line leaving the interviewer shaking his head in disbelief. The point I'm making here is that if you do chose a public figure to illustrate your answer to this question, don't go overboard on your praise for them. Be sure of your facts and figures, history and anything else you wish to use for why you think they are a good leader.

A far safer strategy would be to describe someone your interviewer has never heard of. Far be it from me to encourage you to make use a fictional example...

> I used to work for a manager called Albert Einstein. He was head of a team of eight people including myself. I found him to be an excellent leader because, although he was not the most charismatic person in the world, I trusted him. He was consistent with his treatment of people. When he gave you something to do, you knew what he wanted, how he wanted it and when he expected it by. When he pointed out

something you had failed in it was never in a condescending way and he never shouted at you. He pointed out the error and asked you to come to the conclusion of what the root cause was and then asked what 'we' could do to prevent it happening again. He was loyal to his team but not to the point of blindness. He was always encouraging us to stretch ourselves and do more complex and important tasks. He could definitely keep to himself anything you told him in confidence. He also liked us to have fun at work. He actively encouraged celebrating people's birthdays or the birth of a baby. He was an all round good egg and I wish there were more managers like him. As I progress in my career, I intend to model myself on him.

QUESTIONS ABOUT YOUR CONTINUOUS IMPROVEMENT

If you are applying for any sort of role within a company, particularly in the manufacturing sector, then it is almost certain that you will find yourself being asked questions about 'continuous improvement'. For those who do not know, continuous improvement is a philosophy which does exactly what it says on the tin: it's about looking for changes in the way people do things or processes are performed which provide incremental gains for the organisation. Larger organisations have whole continuous improvement departments where 'lean thinking' and 'just in time' approaches are commonplace. To survive, an organisation must always look to be increasing or maintaining its profits. (Yes, I can hear you say: 'But what about non-profit-making organisations, smarty pants?' These organisations do need to make a profit, perhaps not just in terms of money. Their 'profitability' may be a measure of the impact they make in their field. They will still need to have made a difference compared to their starting point, otherwise what would be the point of their existence?) There are only a limited number of ways to improve profits: sell more, sell at a higher price or spend less on your operations. For the individual employee, the easiest way for them to contribute is in the last area – reducing the cost of what we do.

The Japanese have a word for this philosophy: 'kaizen', which literally translated means 'little – good' demonstrating that the cumulative effect of little actions can have a dramatic effect overall and modern organisations these days recognise that every single employee can contribute to the success of the company no matter what their role. Each employee should be adding value in some way and everyone has a responsibility to contribute to the improvement of the way the business works.

While it may be obvious to those who are at the front line of manufacturing for instance to demonstrate savings made by actions they have taken which have increased productivity, candidates for any position should be ready to provide examples of where they challenged the status quo and made even the smallest of improvements. Below are some examples.

Q Tell us about a time when you initiated an improvement at work.

Office-based example:

I worked for company XYZ Ltd in their purchasing department. In the days before routine ordering via e-mail or the ability to order online, for urgent orders we used to fax them to our suppliers. Now, being a really busy office with many urgent orders, we were sending loads and loads of faxes every day. We had recently had a circular memo reminding us of the costs of leaving lights on etc. and that our telephone bills were really high. I noticed one day that when we were sending faxes, the last page of the order documents often only had a little bit of text at the top and a lot of plain paper underneath. This wasn't planned; it was just the way the text wrapped from one page to the next when it came off the printer. It struck me that every time we sent a fax like that we were paying for a piece of plain paper to go through the fax machine and this was at our expense because the telephone link with the receiver's fax machine was still open. I made a suggestion to the office manager that we tear off any white paper at the end of the fax to use as scrap paper – people used to use Post-it notes for scribbling on – and that way, when the last, short page went through the machine, the fax would cut off and shorten the time we were on the phone line. Now I've no idea how much we saved in terms of the phone bill, but I did see loads of home-made scrap pads from the saved pieces of paper, so it must have been a reasonable amount.

Employers love this type of story. Anything that you have done to save them money translates directly to the bottom line. Each pound/dollar/euro/whatever saved in expenditure is one they can reinvest in the company to secure its future! Never, ever think a small contribution like the one illustrated here would go unnoticed, and it will always earn you brownie points in an interview.

Production-based example:

'When I worked for Mega Crisps Ltd at their potato crisp factory, I was employed as a machine setter. One of my jobs involved removing a circular drum which had around 20 sharp blades in its circumference through which the potatoes passed to be sliced into their final thickness before they were fried, flavoured and bagged. I was instructed to watch a display which showed an ever reducing time reading counting down from four hours down to zero. At that point, I was to remove the drum and replace the blades before putting it back into production. The blades which sliced the potatoes only had a production life of four hours before they became too blunt to slice cleanly. I realised after a bit that I was taking a drum offline, replacing the blades, then putting the drum back into production again. The whole time that this took was around 35 minutes from taking it off to putting it back again. I'd then wait until the next line was due to be dealt with. This might mean a wait of around 45 minutes before the next one was due. I just had to busy myself with cleaning etc., but a lot of the time I was just mooching around waiting to work again. It struck me that if we only had one more drum, I could fill that up with blades while all the machines were operating and then use it to replace the first one as soon as I'd taken it offline. This operation only took five minutes, so the line was only unproductive for five minutes instead of 30. I'd then replace that drum's blades and wait for the next one to require changing and so on and so forth. So over a shift we got an additional 60 minutes of production time for each line. This meant a massive leap in productivity over the year. I got a cash award for that suggestion.

The above was an actual example given to me during an interview. It's a great example because the candidate didn't just follow instructions. He demonstrated a genuine interest in his own job and how he could contribute to the productivity levels. He was directly responsible for increasing the profitability of his organisation and was rightly rewarded for it. Now not everyone will have such an obvious example that they can quote at interview, but I would urge you to think hard about the time when you perhaps acted outside your strict remit and gave that little bit extra for your employer.

Q **Tell us about how you normally cope with a lot of work.**

■ **Where do you start?**

■ **What do you do to ensure it all gets done?**

■ **What prevents you from getting it all done?**

I have deliberately included these questions in the continuous improvement section as good answers to these will demonstrate your ability to recognise and set priorities and be flexible in your approach, all of which show that there is no one answer to any problem and that the ability to make improvements and adjustments to your approach make for a continually improving performance.

I have worked in many roles where I am under pressure to get the work done accurately and on time. I start every morning with a modified 'To Do' list. Apart from being a simple list of things I need to get through, I divide them into four sections: 'Urgent', 'Important', 'Not Urgent' and 'Not Important'. I then look at the tasks and decide which categories they fall into. Of course they can be 'urgent' and 'not important' or 'Important' but 'not urgent' too or any combination, and it's the 'urgent' and 'important' that I work on first, with the 'not important' and 'not urgent' going to the bottom of my list. Of course, a task's status can change at any time and may move up or down the list, so to make it easier for me I have a clipboard permanently marked with the four categories onto which I stick the tasks written on post-it notes. That way its easy to see where any task is in terms of status. When a task is complete, I remove the Post-it from my clipboard.

I ensure it all gets done by referring to the 'expiry date' I write at the bottom of each post-it note and make sure these deadlines are met. At the end of the day I always go over what is left on the board and reconsider their status. If a deadline is looming I may move it into the urgent category for instance.

What prevents me from getting it all done? Well, the usual things, I suppose: telephone calls, e-mails, colleagues and bosses interrupting me! My approach is to try and be disciplined with my time. I will have set times for answering e-mails or making calls where possible, although you have to be flexible too to cope with what the job throws at you.

What you have done here is demonstrated an excellent grasp of time-management skills – as taught by many reputable and fine organisations. Even if you don't employ such techniques, at least be aware of them so that you might quote them in the interview situation.

QUESTIONS ABOUT YOUR CUSTOMER AWARENESS

Q What, in your view, makes it difficult to relate well to certain customers?

This question is typical of the approach many interviewers take nowadays. Instead of asking questions that allow you to demonstrate how easy it is for you to do your job and how wonderful everyone thinks you are, the questions concentrate on what some might consider as 'failures' or at least times when things haven't gone so well. Again, fear not, as it gives you a chance to show how resilient you are and how flexible and adaptable you are.

For this question you should be focusing on the fact that customers come in all shapes, sizes and types and that there will be, on occasion, times when you encounter a customer that you don't naturally 'gel' with.

On occasion I have had to deal with a shouty, irate, greedy and downright rude customer. While inside I might feel mortified and offended at their behaviour, I realise that I have to be professional and maintain a calm demeanour. I allow them to rant and raise their voice for a bit and at all times I keep my voice on an even level. I allow them to blow themselves out. I don't take their views personally because it's not me they are really having a go at, but their frustration is being vented at me, as the public voice/face of the company. I would never react like that to a similar situation, so I cannot really understand what motivates them to be so awful. So while I may not be able to relate to them on that level, at least I can still deal with them in a way that I know is professional and hopefully will resolve the problem.

Q Tell me about a recent situation when you had to build a relationship with a new customer.

For all customer-facing roles you can almost guarantee that this question will come up. A business can only grow in two ways. The first is by selling more to existing customers. (This can be difficult – the amount they purchase from you is determined by factors totally beyond your control. Growth in sales to existing customers tends to be a slow process. Imagine it like the relationship between a man and a woman. At first the gifts come thick and fast before levelling out to being just at Christmas, birthdays and special occasions...). The second is by increasing the sales base by attracting new customers.

What the interviewer does not want to hear is an account of your fantastic cold-calling skills and how many new customers you attracted by sheer strength of your personality. Rather they are looking for a specific instance where you secured a sale with a notoriously reticent customer or where the sale was a direct result of YOUR efforts.

I remember a time a few months ago when I received an enquiry from a local business relating to a product we stocked. This gentleman had very specific needs and was able to quote the exact specification of the item almost as if he had designed the thing. I calmly noted down his enquiry and took his number so that I could call him back. Aware that this could lead to bigger and better things, I asked HIM what would be the best time to call him back with the price and delivery information he needed. I could've actually given him his answers there and then, but I wanted to run past my supervisor first my idea about giving this new customer our top-level discount and having the part taken over to him that day. After all, I thought, if it had been an existing customer, we'd have only made the smaller margin anyway, and in terms of the cost of same day delivery, it was a 'sprat to catch a mackerel'. I'm pleased to say that the customer was delighted and we got lots of new business from him afterwards. I made sure though in the early days it was only me who dealt with him in order to build a sustainable relationship with the customer. I suppose you could say it was because that I took personal responsibility for us keeping our promises to him. I was even aware later on that some of the items we supplied to him he could have sourced elsewhere locally a bit cheaper, but obviously the good service was what mattered to him the most.'

Its clever to put this last bit in, as all companies would like to pride themselves on their level of customer service, and would see themselves in you by your obviously highly developed customer service skills!

Q Give me an example when you have given excellent customer service.

Again, the temptation here is to cite some example where you climbed up to the summit of Mount Everest, sought out the expedition leader and said: 'Here, you left your change on the counter!' Interviewers are realistic (honest) so a more mundane example of where you just did that little bit extra and helped someone's day be that little bit better is perfectly acceptable here.

We received a request in our office for an application form for an office role we had advertised. One of the guys came in from the shop floor with his greasy overalls and mucky hands to collect one. He was a bit self-conscious given the nature of the role he was applying for was white collar and he had always been a blue collar worker. During the process of getting the blank form I chatted to him the whole time telling him how good it was that he was applying and how he would stand a good chance of getting it with his experience in the company etc. As well as giving him the form, I gave him an A4 envelope so he wouldn't need to fold the form, and then put the whole shebang into a bigger envelope so the stuff wouldn't get dirty from his hands. The look on his face made me realise that I had made a good impression on him. This was backed up later after he didn't get the job when he popped in to see me to say thanks for the support.

Nothing earth shattering, but a touching little story which shows your skills.

QUESTIONS ABOUT YOUR DECISION-MAKING SKILLS AND JUDGEMENT

Questions like these are used in every context, however junior the position may be that you are applying for. We all have to make decisions every day and it's the methodology of how you reach your conclusion on how to act that the interviewer is looking for here. As much as you may think you have a natural innate skill and are getting it right, the reality is that you WILL follow some form of logical process in your mind before you make a decision.

There are no right and wrong answers here, but my top tip for you is to realise that different forms of decision-making are appropriate for different sets of circumstances. It may well be that in an ideal world you would sit down and gather all the facts in front of you and weigh each one up carefully before modelling possible outcomes and consequences of each route you might take before deciding on the one course of action that offers the least risk/biggest return etc., but life being what it is you will sometimes have to make decisions based on gut instinct or incomplete facts. It's how you treat this situation and how you react to the result that is important here. As I have said elsewhere in this book, do not be afraid to share an experience that was less than happy in its outcome. If you can demonstrate a lesson learned you will have demonstrated both resilience and the ability to progress to your interviewer, and both of these qualities will earn you big Brownie points!

Q **Tell us about a recent situation in which you had to be reach a decision without having all the facts.**

Although this example may seem trivial, it demonstrates maturity and an ability to approach work conceptually. The interviewer will want to know that you understand that just getting the job done isn't enough. Your response should show resourcefulness and initiative.

When I was on work placement from university, my supervisor, a marketing manager, asked me to assemble five hundred press kits for a mailing. I wasn't sure in what order the pages and press releases should go, but my supervisor had already left for a client meeting. Afraid of putting the information together in the wrong order, I managed to track down her mobile phone number and called her in her car. She explained the order of the materials over the phone, and in the end I managed to prevent a mistake that would have cost hours of work and a delay in the mailing – not to mention a few headaches.

Q How do you usually go about solving a problem?

The interviewer will want to hear the logic you use to solve problems as well as the outcomes you're able to achieve. Are you decisive? How do you narrow the options and make decisions? What do people say about your reasoning skills?

When I need to solve a problem, I often start by writing down as many ideas as I can think of about possible causes. Next I look for relationships among the causes so I can group together symptoms of bigger problems. Usually, after I study these groups of problems, the real cause becomes readily apparent. I can then devise a route to getting a resolution.

Q Would you say you are good at making decisions?

It's time once more to admit your fallibility I'm afraid. There is not a single one of us who has not made a decision in our lives that has turned out to be the wrong one. This answer is short and sweet, but irrefutable.

I do have my own preferred style of making decisions and that is, like most people I guess, in circumstances where all the facts are to hand and I have enough time to weigh up the options properly and then come to a reasoned decision. That is not always possible of course and sometimes we have to go with what's available. We've all made decisions which turned out to be the wrong one. Hindsight is 20–20 vision after all. However, I hope that any wrong decision I have made in the past has left its mark on me so that I can learn from it and avoid making the same mistake again.

QUESTIONS ABOUT YOUR INFLUENCING SKILLS

For the vast majority of us, our ability to make things happen through other people will come from being able to influence them rather than by our directing them. While we all may work in organisations that are hierarchical in structure, the stark reality is that most changes of direction come through decisions being made following acceptance of a point of view from individuals requiring the changes to be made. That's not to say that there are no direct 'chain of command' decisions, it's just that these tend to be for the more formal, strategic or tactical decisions, not the minutae of everyday workplace life.

Think of it this way: where would we be without lies in our society? Your immediate thought might be 'in a much better world'. Would we? It's the little lies which are recognised by all but acknowledged by no one that oil the wheels of our social transactions. How many marriages would still be intact if the truthful answer to the question 'Does my bum look big in this?' were given? We are all subject to influence from our subordinates, peers and superiors at work without the need for formal orders being given or followed. While there are some roles which will obviously require you to have a fair amount of influencing skills – sales staff, marketing people, etc. – enlightened employers will recognise too that there may be occasions where you need to get things done by others when, strictly speaking, you don't have the authority to demand or instruct them to be done. For example, production people will always be at odds with maintenance people due to the conflicting agendas they have: production will always be wishing to produce, while maintenance will always seek to have production stopped in order for maintenance to be carried out properly. So, as you can see, you have probably applied for a position where your ability to influence others is an important part of your job – whether it is in the job description or not!

Q **What are your strengths in terms of influencing people?**

■ **What's your approach in influencing others?**

■ **What could you do to make yourself more effective in influencing others?**

I think the strength I have in influencing others lies within my ability to communicate well with others in order to get them to share my vision of what success looks like. I have found that people are on the whole suspicious of anything which effects change without their understanding of the thought processes behind the decision which would result in change. Its simply impractical to involve everyone in every decision-making process; what I like to do is to take the time to reiterate the current state, then say why the changes are necessary. I give a broad-brush picture of what was being thought about when a solution was being worked out and tell them of the reasons why I or we decided on a particular course of action. I'd then describe what likely results would come out of this change and I would be sure to make them feel that they were recognised as important in the achievement of the new objective and thank them in advance for them helping out. I think I could improve my influencing skills if I slowed down a little bit. Sometimes in my enthusiasm I skip over points that to me are obvious, but to the person I'm talking to might not be. I sometimes then have to backtrack to explain what I meant on some points. Maybe I could plan my discussion with them better. Maybe I could write out some bullet points to make sure I covered all the bases.

The final element in this answer shows that you are human. As I've said earlier, employers far prefer to see a candidate who has a high level of self-awareness and knows their development needs than to interview someone who is so smug that they never admit to having made a mistake in the past or need to change in any way.

Q Give an example of when you had to settle a dispute between two people.

There were two colleagues within my section whose relationship deteriorated to the point where the atmosphere was terrible. As they couldn't resolve it, I decided to see what I could do. My aim was to first take any heat out of the situation by calming down the individuals. Then I arranged a three-way discussion later in the day away from the section in a meeting room so we wouldn't be disturbed. I made sure that I was in charge of the discussion of the issues, the reason being to arrive at an agreed positive way of going forward or a compromise. I think it's important to understand each person's standpoint and feelings, without necessarily agreeing with them. It wasn't pretty at first, with both of them just trying to score points. But I suppose I used my diplomatic skills to get them to see that there was no future in the current situation and that a compromise was the only possible solution. After about an hour, we left the room with a shaky compromise, but I made sure that whenever possible afterwards I encouraged them to be first more civil, then in time more friendly towards each other. The result was an easing of the atmosphere and then a return to normal.

Q Have you ever had a conflict with a superior? How was it resolved?

Yes, I have had conflicts in the past. Never major ones, but certainly there have been situations where there was a disagreement that needed to be resolved. I've found that when conflict occurs, it's because of a failure to see both sides of the situation. Therefore I ask the other person to give me their perspective and at the same time ask that they allow me to fully explain my perspective. At that point, I would work with the person to find out if a compromise could be reached. If not, I would submit to their decision because they are my superior. In the end, you have to be willing to submit yourself to the directives of your superiors, whether you're in full agreement or not.

Q **Some people are easier to persuade than others. Which people do you find it hard to persuade?**

■ **What is it that makes persuading them so difficult?**

I think the people I find most hard to persuade are people who have opinions based solely on prejudice or bias. People who are bigoted, racist, misogynistic, etc. can often have views that are so entrenched that they are unlikely ever to change. I think you have to make a judgement call as to whether or not it is really your place to attempt to change these people, or whether or not you have to accept that while you may disagree strongly with their views, you might still have to work with them. Of course, you might be forced into a situation where you have to confront someone about their views if it is against your employer's dignity and diversity policy for instance, but you can still ask them politely to keep such views to themselves in the working environment. I think you have to develop your own skills in deciding when enough is enough-when you are not going to get that sale, when you are not going to convince your boss to give you that rise, or when it's simply time to stop banging your head against a brick wall!

This answer conveys some good points. It shows that you are aware that you can never change the world entirely, that you can employ diplomatic skills when necessary, and that you can also cry 'enough!' when it is warranted.

QUESTIONS ABOUT YOUR DEVELOPMENT OF SELF AND OTHERS

Q What do you consider to be your weaknesses?

Time and again, this question proves to be the one interviewees most dread. I bet you've heard it before, and I bet you hated it! In the many, many years in which I have asked this particular question, it is the one that most often provokes a 'rabbit caught in headlights' look.

Take heart, because all is not lost! You do not need to launch into a list of your failings and foibles, exposing your lack of self-worth and insecurities and ultimately giving your interviewer a hundred and one reasons NOT to employ you!

Perhaps you would feel more comfortable if it were couched like this:

Q What would you consider to be your development needs?

Now doesn't that sound better? I can hear you breathe out as you read this new, more touchy-feely version of the old classic. In fact, they are exactly the same question and really designed to illicit the same kind of answer. Think of it like this: why would an interviewer expect you to tell him something about you that absolutely rules you out of getting the job? It wouldn't make any sense. It would be asking you to prove a negative. An interviewer's job is not only to find out if the candidate is the best fit for the job now, but also to see if they can grow within the company and expand on their existing skills and ultimately become a more valuable asset to the company.

A good answer to this question might be:

I'm glad you asked me that. I periodically take time to review my skills and recently I thought I might like to expand my commercial knowledge a little. I thought perhaps a more formal training course in business finance might compliment my general commercial awareness. Also, I have found that recent developments in software package XYZ may help me be more productive. Perhaps I will buy a manual on the subject or go on a refresher course.

The key is never to come across too cocky as if you have nothing new to learn. We can all do with at least some refresher training in at least one aspect of our skill set. How long ago was it since you qualified? If the company you are hoping to work for has an international dimension, perhaps you'd like to learn a new language. When was the last time you used the more obscure functions of a spreadsheet programme? Are you really Mary Poppins? (Practically perfect in every way.) No, probably not.

Do not be afraid of this question. It is one that you are very, very likely to be asked at interview, so be prepared for it. Think of something you are reasonably good at (at least good enough for the job as it's been described to you) and then decide how you could be even better at it. It is better to have over-capacity of skill than under.

Q In what past situations have you been most effective in developing others?

This question is aimed at determining your ability to act outside of your own personal silo. If you have occupied roles in the past where it was part of your responsibilities to develop others, then all well and good. Draw upon those experiences to highlight a good example of developing someone – perhaps illustrating how their appraisal rating improved following your help. If not, then you should be thinking about occasions when, through sheer generosity of spirit of course, you went out of your way to help someone improve or progress, for example:

*I remember the time when one of our more junior members of staff
was struggling to get to grips with the human resource software we
had. She had been given the usual training that we all had and a
photocopied manual. To be honest, the manual was like one of those
flat-pack instruction booklets, and not much good to anyone really.
She was the type of person who didn't like to complain and
occasionally took flak for mistakes she had made. I took her to one side
and asked if I could assist. We agreed that for half an hour each
lunchtime I would sit with her and we would go through the parts of
the package that she was less than sure about. In the end it took about
two or three weeks, but I was happy to help her and she rarely made
mistakes like she had before again. On my birthday she bought me a
big bunch of flowers to say thank you. I was really made up!*

Remember, interviewers very rarely ask a single question and let you answer
it fully before moving onto the next one. They may wish to drill down into
what you've initially told them, so be prepared for this. For example:

Q What did you do specifically that was effective?

*Having known this girl for a short time, I knew that if she was pointed
towards our training department for help it wouldn't work because
she'd see it as a sign of failure, and that others were recognising her
shortcomings. By lending a hand in an informal way, it was less of a
big deal and she responded to that. If anything, it was me who plonked
myself down beside her each day with my sandwiches so she couldn't
go anywhere until we had her knowledge at the level she needed to be
successful. So I suppose you could say it was my persistence and my
approach that was effective.*

Q What was the last piece of learning you undertook?

Now instantly you are thinking back to the last formal course or
qualification you took. In the words of George Gershwin, 'It aint necessarily

so! Most professional institutions such as the Chartered Institute for Personnel and Development require their members to demonstrate continuing professional development and cite reading articles and books, watching TV shows, attending lectures or seminars, secondments, etc. as just as legitimate learning experiences as the more traditional types of learning such as courses of study which lead to a qualification.

This might be a typical answer:

> *I was watching the news only the other evening and there was a piece on the new anti-smoking legislation coming into force in England and what it would mean for employers. It struck me that there had been no discussion about this at work and it made me think we might be unprepared for what was coming. I went onto the Internet and downloaded the actual statutory instrument as well as all the comments on the ACAS and DTI websites and I also looked at discussion forums. I then took all this information to the HR officer. I was right. We were unprepared and I have been co-opted onto a committee which is looking at all the aspects of the legislation and we are tasked with coming up with policies and proposals for practical measures to make sure we comply.*

Don't for a second think that this will make you look like a swot. Employers are desperate to find people who are prepared to 'go the extra mile' for them and use their own imagination and creativity to resolve problems and issues. This type of answer demonstrates to the interviewer that the candidate has an awareness of the bigger picture, a bit of get-up-and-go to do the research, and a willingness to help colleagues from other departments.

QUESTIONS ABOUT YOUR TEAMWORKING SKILLS

For the vast majority of us, we will during our employment be required to work as part of a team. This may be a small unit of two or three people; alternatively it may be a larger team altogether. Good management practice has it that the maximum number of people any one person can manage well is around 12–15. If the number is any higher than this, then there is usually simply not enough time to devote to each team member to get the best out of them. Conversely, a manager should be able to spend more time with their team the smaller the number of members. Its in everyone's interest that a team performs well. It should perform better than a simple sum of its parts. A good team is made up of people with an array of talents which compliment each other. After all, you couldn't field a cup-winning team of 11 strikers or 11 goalkeepers! Your interviewer will probably already have a good idea of the attributes of those in the team for which they are recruiting for and will be looking to see if you possess the necessary complimentary attributes. Its easy and glib to say 'Oh yes, I'm a good team player' but what does that actually mean? Let me give you some killer responses to these types of questions.

Q **Tell us about the last time you worked as part of a team.**

■ **What did you like about working in the group?**

■ **What did you dislike?**

The last time I worked as part of a team was when I worked for XYZ Co. I was part of a team in a call centre which sold new and renewed existing motor and home insurance policies. The team I worked in was around 10 or 12 in number and the group was fairly stable with not many starters or leavers. I really appreciated the fact that the team was made up of a diverse range of people in terms of their age, their background, their ethnicity and character. I felt it gave us a rounded view of things because of the variety of life views. There were some who were experts in the home market and some who were experts in the motor market. We were encouraged to share tips and tricks with each other and to bond as a team socially as well. I suppose the selling type environment would foster a strong team anyway, but I think it was more than that. When we socialised we always made it as inclusive as possible. For example, a couple of members of my team were Muslim girls and couldn't go into pubs, so we made sure that we didn't always suggest drinking as a social activity. I honestly believe that our closeness as a team of individuals made us better as a team collectively. What did I dislike? Well I think that sometimes it can be harder to be recognised for any special efforts you have made personally and that maybe you could get lost in the crowd a bit. Although, I think its probably down to the individual at their annual appraisal not to be shy in demonstrating what they've done well. I wouldn't say there's too much not to like about working in a team for me, maybe its not for everyone, but I thrive in that environment.

Q Tell me about a time when you had to get people to work together more supportively.

- ■ What caused the original difficulties?
- ■ How did the others respond to you?
- ■ What would you do differently next time?

These type of questions may appear to be aimed at people who control the activities of team members, i.e. supervisors. However – and remember this because it is a truism not widely understood – while there may be a titular head of a team, there are also the unsung or unrecognised leaders of teams. These are those who, through respect from their peers or by a natural ability, actually influence the work of others. These people are often natural coaches and mentors, and while they may not have any leadership type of job title on their contract, are as much a driving force behind a team's performance as their appointed leader. So, even if you have not held a leadership position, you may be able to describe instances where you influenced others.

I remember this time at XYZ Co. when I was working as part of a team who were brought together to plan and execute an office move to another building. The management thought it was a good idea to get people involved from all areas of the company, although some cynics said it was to get it done on the cheap rather than hiring a specialist firm. I tend to think that the management were enlightened enough to think that the whole experience might just be good in terms of the team members' personal development as well as tapping into the existing talent pool. We were led by a manager who had had some experience in project management and the firm didn't appear to be taking too big a risk by appointing her. In the early meetings I was aware that we were going through a normal process of jostling for position, trying to 'bags' the better tasks of the project and finding our niche in the whole thing. I know from my studies of group dynamics that new teams go through a stage of 'storming' initially, they then settle and find their shape in the 'forming' phase and then work unconsciously and consciously together in a stage known as 'norming', that is they all work to the same standards. I was acutely aware that our project leader, while very hot on detail and the mechanics of project management, failed to recognise what I was seeing which was that people were being paired up to work on elements of the move in a very haphazard way. She was not taking notice of what's people's backgrounds were or attempting to play to their strengths. After a while it became clear that a number of people in the team were really quite unhappy and when I asked them if they had brought it to our project leader's attention, they said they didn't want to upset her or rock the boat. After I realised that around half the team of 12 were unhappy I took what was, I suppose, a risky step. I called a private meeting of them and we aired our grievances to one another. Now this could have been a pretty unproductive activity if I hadn't made a point of going round the table and getting everyone to say what they would rather be doing and why they felt they were right for it. As it turned out, we were able to produce a proposal to shuffle people round in order that they may contribute more fully – for example, one team member was tasked with dealing with the telephone provider over the arrangements for our telephony requirements in the new place yet she had a background in sales. She swapped with one of the IT guys who was happy to take it on. She ended up negotiating with removal men over the costs of the move. Once we had an alternate plan I arranged to meet the project leader privately. I broached the subject carefully saying how this was not an attempt to undermine her authority, but, realising how busy she was, it was an effort on my part to take to her a solution, not just a problem. She was taken aback a little at first, but I talked her round into seeing the plan's advantages and she then ratified the changes at the next team meeting. What would I do differently? I probably would have had the guts to approach her myself much earlier on, because on reflection, it maybe did seem to appear a bit rebellious on my part.

THE '...AND FINALLY' QUESTIONS

One of the reasons that human resources has occasionally received a hard time over the years was the propensity of some of its practitioners to put questions the purpose of which the interviewee couldn't understand, nor could they see how what they might give as an answer would have any relevance to the role they had applied for.

We have already seen that one of the factors in successful performance in a role is the ability of the post holder to assimilate into the culture of the organisation, or at least to 'fit in' with those around them. Therefore it would be a legitimate aim of any interviewer to get an impression of the kind of person the candidate is in terms of character, interests, etc. Of course, the interviewer may just be nosey!

What follows are what I call the '... and finally' questions. I have named these after the more frivolous news items that came at the end of news bulletins in the UK. If you are asked these types of questions, they will most likely come at the end of the interview. Obviously there are no right or wrong answers to these questions, only your own answers.

Here are some for you to consider what kind of answer you might give:

Q **What would constitute a perfect evening for you?**

Q **What would be a nightmare evening?**

Q **Would you rather have an extremely successful professional life and have a tolerable home life, or have a fabulous home life and a merely tolerable professional life?**

Q If you could wake up tomorrow having gained one new ability, skill or quality, what would it be?

Q Who is your hero/heroine (alive or dead)?

Q Who is your biggest villain?

Q Describe the one person who has had the single biggest influence on your life.

Q Has anyone told you that you have been their inspiration?

Q How forgiving are you? Give me an example.

Q Have you ever made a big sacrifice? If you have, is it something you have kept to yourself or do others know about it?

Q Has anyone ever made a big sacrifice for you?

Q What percentage of people your age do you think are having a better life than you? On a scale of 1 to 10, how happy are you?

Q Tell me about the last time you laughed at yourself.

Q Do others laughing at you bother you?

CHAPTER 7

QUESTIONS YOU CAN ASK AT YOUR INTERVIEW

During the vast majority of assessment or interview processes you will be given the opportunity to ask questions of the recruiters. While your brain may be shouting to you to ask questions like 'How much filthy lucre are you gonna pay me big boy?' or 'So exactly how big is my private office going to be?' you should be aware that on where you are in the recruitment process will depend what questions from you will be appropriate.

For example, you have been called for a first-stage interview. Your letter has clearly defined that this is an 'initial stage in the process'. It would be completely inappropriate to ask questions relating to remuneration at this stage. What follows is a brief guide to the types of questions you can ask at each stage.

FIRST-ROUND INTERVIEWS

Questions at this stage from you will be directed squarely at the nature of the employer's business and the role for which you are applying. For example:

Q I see that Company XYZ made an operating profit of £Xm last year [good opportunity to show off your research on them if they haven't given you a chance to do so up to now]. Can you share with me any projections for this operating year?'

I have deliberately used the word 'share' here as it shows them that you are aware that this is potentially sensitive information. It gives them an out if they can't tell you this type of information without it being an awkward moment. You should be asking this question to get a feel what the overall prospects are for this company. After all, you don't want to join a firm that makes umbrellas when we are heading for ten years of drought!

Q What does the company do by way of developing its employees?

This question is the polar opposite of the classic question they might ask you on where you see yourself in five years time. Depending on your role, further development may not be a must for you. However, be aware that many professional organisations require their members to demonstrate continuing professional development (CPD) and a firm which would not give you the opportunity to do this would not be good for your longer-term career prospects. It is possible that the organisation may not have a robust system in place for identifying talent within and developing it further. Gauge their response carefully as they may waffle on a bit about how training is always available to fit the needs of the company etc. You should be able to tell if it's a sincere answer or not. Alternatively, completely turn it back on them by asking:

Q Where would you see ME in five years time?'

or

Q Has this role been included in any succession planning?

One of the biggest sources of unease in employment is when you are in a position of uncertainty about your performance. Not all people managers are good people managers, and they may not make their subordinates aware of the expectations they have of them. Many people have told me that they resent the annual appraisal meeting, especially if they are criticised for under performing during the year but have had no indication during that year that they were failing. Try this question:

Q What would outstanding performance in this role look like?

Once they have answered this question, you will at least know how high you have to aim for!

Q What are the reporting lines within this organisation?

Many organisations will not describe the structure of the organisation either in the initial advertisement or in the papers they subsequently send you prior to the interview. In many cases, an invitation will consist of a letter detailing where and when you have to present yourself and who you are going to meet. Of course you may have had the foresight to request a Job Description before the interview anyway, but if you haven't then it's not too late at the interview to get this point clarified if your interviewer hasn't described the set-up to you.

FINAL-STAGE INTERVIEW

All your hard work and preparation for the first interview has paid off and they've asked you back for a final look at you. It may well be that they want you to jump through more hoops such as delivering a presentation or completing psychometric tests as well as a face-to-face interview. I will leave it to other publications to counsel you on these aspects of recruitment so here we will dwell on your proactive contribution to this 'conversation'.

If you have been wise, you will have done further research into the company, its business and the market it operates in. You will be aware of the trends and threats to their operation. You will, in short, be a good person for them to choose to deliver a presentation on their company, so in-depth will your knowledge of them be! Now is the time for you to ask them questions that not only elicit answers from them that assist you in making your decision about whether or not you want to work for them, but also demonstrate your understanding of your research and also what was said to you during the initial interview. This is the time to also get a flavour of what it is actually like to be an employee of Company XYZ.

Some examples:

Q You mentioned when we first met that the company was expanding into Eastern Europe. What does this mean for the UK operation?

Q At our first meeting you said that there were no plans to further mechanise your operation. Given that most European firms cannot compete with Far Eastern manufacturers on price because their labour costs are so low, can this lack of mechanisation be a long-term strategy, or is it subject to change?

Q What is your employee turnover level?

Q What were the headline results of your last employee satisfaction survey?

Q Why do people like working here?

Q How would you describe the atmosphere and culture within this organisation?

CHAPTER 8
AFTER THE INTERVIEW

LEARNING FROM REJECTION

You were convinced that this was going to be it. You had been looking around for a while, but no jobs seemed to be advertised that suited your unique mix of skills and abilities. When you saw your dream job advertised at last, you really felt like this was it. So after toiling away on your covering letter and CV and tailoring the information to fit what the recruiter seemed to be looking for, you sent your application in and, sure enough, you were called for a first-round interview.

And you could tell that the interviewers really liked you. So, you were not surprised when they called you back for a second-stage interview. You were ready for it. It was kismet after all. Then they asked you to have a tour of the company. You knew that you were a finalist, and you were starting to think about salary questions, benefits and the like. You even started looking at new cars, thinking about how you could get one that was less than ten years old at last.

And then the phone call came. 'I'm sorry to have to tell you this,' the voice began. Somewhere beyond your disappointment, you knew you had to finish the conversation, but what were you going to say and how were you going to handle it?

This all sounds a little dramatic I suppose, but, for those of you who have already been out in the job market, I'm sure some of it also sounds familiar. And it soon will be for those of you about to go out into the market. Given the number of people who apply for all positions these days, the fact is that the odds are that you could well face some kind of rejection before you finally land the job that you want.

For all that has been written about getting a job in a difficult economy, and for all of the advice that you have probably received from friends and family, not much is said about dealing with the other side of coin – about not getting the job.

Although rejection happens so often in the crowded job market, there is still a strange kind of denial about it. It is one of those ugly realities that only seem approachable through statistics and ratios that compare applicants to openings.

Post-graduate placement programmes, for example, tend to focus on the positive. They want you to hope for the best and make their graduates believe in their chances, so they may not spend time talking about worst-case scenarios or how to deal with bad news. But you should take a moment to think about rejection. How will you respond if you do not get the job? How you handle that scenario can be as important as what you say or do during an interview.

Some forms of rejection are less painful than others. If you applied for a position and never made it to the interview stage, receiving a rejection letter in the post may be disappointing but it isn't usually devastating. After all, the recruiter never saw you face to face. They don't know what you are like or how you conduct yourself in a professional conversation. They have not seen you work or heard you speak passionately about your achievements.

In short, they have not rejected you personally and, conversely, you have not had the chance to size them up and get a sense of how you would fit in with the department and the organisation as a whole. In a sense, it has all been a paper transaction.

All the recruiter knows of you is what's on your cover letter and CV, so, if you want to think about this constructively, your attention should be focused on those materials. Did you tailor your cover letter to meet the needs and requirements as they were set out in the job ad or did you send a generic cover letter? Have you honestly assessed your CV and given serious thought as to how you could make it more competitive and more enticing? Do you need more experience? Could you be more active professionally? Do you need to gain a higher profile in your field? Do you need to get more involved in professional organisations?

Now, say that you do make it past the application stage. You are called in for an interview but, alas, do not get the job. The sense of personal rejection is far more acute and the emotional consequences more severe.

In a competitive market, getting an interview is a feat that can actually make you believe, often cruelly, that you might get the job. The odds have dramatically improved in your favour; where you were 1 of 150, now you are 1 of 5 or 10.

As calm and collected as you might try to be about it all, you might not be able to help daydreaming about job offers or planning your future with the firm. And, since what largely determines whether you move on or go home is how you present yourself and your performance during this process, it is hard not to take a rejection at this stage of the game personally and not to feel that somehow they just did not like you.

Rejected after an interview, your initial impulse may well be to return the blow that you have been dealt in some way, shape or form. If someone does call to give you the news, you may feel like telling them 'Huh! I didn't really want your stupid job anyway!' in a ya-boo-sucks kind of way. Or if they have notified you by post, you may be inclined to send them a scathing letter in return that burns a hole through their ink blotters and forces them into a life of watching daytime TV and listening to old Gary Glitter records.

But, while it may make you feel better temporarily, with every damning word and every seething syllable, you will, in more ways than one, be cutting your own throat, professionally speaking. An emotional outburst after a rejection can make navigating a tight job market all the more complicated, awkward and difficult, because you may have to see or work with these people again in some other professional capacity. It is amazing how small some of these disciplines can actually get. You may suddenly spot a member of the recruitment panel on a committee at a professional conference or see them in the audience when you deliver a speech. It could be that you run across them again in a more mundane capacity. Either way, its going to be excruciatingly embarrassing for you!

Networking is part of many jobs, so, by offending a recruiter, you could also be offending a network and burning more bridges than you realise. And (yes there's another 'and'), even though you have been rejected for the job in question, you never really know how things will work out. New starts do not always stay put or keep their jobs. Some simply do not fit in as well as the recruiters thought that they would. Others move on after a short while because their dream job was something else or somewhere else. In addition, departments often find themselves with sudden retirements or extended leaves of absence. If you had just recruited for a position and had an excellent first choice but another really good candidate and you suddenly had to hire for the role again, where would you look first?

If getting your dream job is like winning the lottery, then maybe the catchphrase still applies: 'You can't win it unless you're in it.'

And though you may be inclined to believe that they did this to you just to see you suffer, the fact is that recruiters are people, too. Not too long ago, they were sitting in a similar seat, dealing with the same stress and responding to the same types of questions. They probably hate rejecting you just as much as you hate being rejected. They have also had to give up their valuable time to conduct the recruitment process.

Your anger, your bitterness and your insults will not mortally wound them or make them change their minds and realise the error of their ways. In the end, it will only confirm their decision to reject you.

For all of the negatives that go along with being rejected, then, there still can be some positive spin-offs. Whether it leads to a job down the road or it adds to your list of contacts or not, you should still try to think about the experience in constructive terms, in the same way that you would revise your cover letter and CV for future searches.

Make a note of questions that you had difficulty with or questions that stood out in your mind. Also, make a list of questions that you could have asked. Think about how you handled yourself and how you prepared. Were you able to effectively elaborate on the information that you provided in your initial application? Did you do some research on the company before you were interviewed? If you think that your interview skills need work, then you might want to set up a mock interview or make an appointment with a careers adviser to talk about how you conduct yourself through the process. You could also consult with your careers adviser if you had questions about what you said or did during the interview itself.

The interview process does not, and should not, end just because you were rejected. In a sense, the rejection is still a part of the interview. It gives you yet another chance to demonstrate your maturity, to show your understanding of the profession and the hiring process, and to prove to the recruiter that you are a worthy candidate, even if you are not its first choice. It certainly is a possibility that you should be ready for, because, depending upon how you handle it, it could conceivably be that situation that makes it your year after all.

Of course, if you DO put into practice some or all of the techniques I have outlined in this book, then this chapter may not be of any use to you at all!

RESIGNING FROM YOUR CURRENT JOB

Phew! You've done it! You've done all your research and put your time in getting ready for that final interview. You dazzled the interviewers with your intelligence, charm, wit and they were gagging to hire you. You've negotiated your terms and you've accepted the job offer and there's only one thing left to do: resign from your current job.

The first thing you should do is tell your current manager. While you will definitely hand over a formal letter (won't you? That's right – keep thinking 'I am a professional'), but before that you should sit down face to face and let your manager know informally.

Make sure you prepare what you're going to say beforehand and try and guess your manager's reaction. You should be positive about your time in that role and be grateful for the opportunities you've been given while you were there. Try to remain calm, professional and polite and, no matter how tempting it is, resist the urge to get personal!

Once you've let your manager know verbally, you should hand over a typed resignation letter. If you wish, hand it over there and then; if you feel more comfortable, then deliver it later that day by hand.

In your letter you should include the position you are resigning from and the date you intend to leave. Although not essential, you might want to repeat your thanks for the opportunities you have been given and offer your willingness to ensure a smooth handover to your successor.

While a little constructive criticism is acceptable, for example if your career aspirations have been frustrated by your employer's lack of recognition of your talents, don't get personal or you'll risk your reference and your reputation.

Always stick to the reasons you've given for leaving. Telling your manager one thing and your co – workers another risks compromising your professionalism and making your last few weeks feel awkward.

If you've done everything a loyal employee is expected to have done and you've performed well in your role, the chances are your organisation won't want to see you go. The most likely way an employer will try and make you stay is by offering you a pay rise either equal to or above what you've been offered in your new job.

You should take any counter offer they make you seriously and carefully consider how you would feel about staying in the same job but with a better salary. This may help remind you of the other reasons you have for leaving and help you make your decision.

Employers may also try to get you to stay by promising you a promotion and increased responsibility. Again, you should think carefully about what this means but don't forget that you'll be working in the same organisation, with the same people and probably under the same manager.

Whatever the length of your notice period, you're legally obliged to work it, unless your employer is willing to waive it. Look at your written contract of employment, you should find details of your notice period there. Otherwise, you should allow between two weeks and a month. Be aware that the remedy an employer has against an employee who does not work their notice is to try to recover any losses they may sustain or claim damages against you in a court of law. Now, the nature of your role and how important you are to the organisation will determine the employer's willingness to resort to litigation.

It's easy to imagine your notice period as a time to relax and stop making an effort, but this shouldn't be the case. You'll likely have plenty to keep you busy, finalising any outstanding work and ensuring you properly handover your responsibilities. What's more, being seen to make the effort right up until your last day will ensure your reputation as a professional and reliable employee remains intact. And you never know when you might deal with your employer again.

Make sure you allow time to say goodbye to everyone and swap contact details with as many colleagues as you can. Moving jobs is a great way to extend your network and you may find you see some of your colleagues again sooner than you think.

Don't feel guilty about resigning. Feel good! Working is the nature of business and job mobility is part of business.

While others may think you're resigning from a perfectly good job, you're the one in control of your career and only you can decide which direction it should take. If resigning from your job will bring you closer to meeting your goals, then it's a legitimate step on your career path.

Now go and enjoy your new role!

CHAPTER 9

TELEPHONE INTERVIEWS

Telephone interviews are being used more and more these days as they are extremely time efficient for the recruiter. Once used only by recruitment agencies, many private organisations use these as an initial filter. Undoubtedly you will come across these at some stage in your career, so it's best to have some idea what to expect beforehand.

Think about what you are trying to achieve here. It's not about actually securing the job at this stage. It's about getting to the next level which involves a face to face interview

Everything I have said previously about you doing research on the organisation still applies. The advantage you will have this time is that you can have all your research notes in front of you to refer to, rather than having to commit it all to memory. This goes for your CV and covering letter too. Have them in easy reach. Even better, why not prepare a reference sheet with points to jog your memory on specific tasks you have worked on, achievements you have made or projects you've taken part in?

When you agree to an appointment for a telephone interview, make sure that you choose a time where you know you can definitely be in an environment conducive to you giving your best. That means no interruptions, no background noise, etc. If you can, make sure you receive the call on a landline. Then there is no worry about batteries going flat or reception being lost. You will be more likely to be relaxed and give a better account of yourself in this type of environment.

The biggest drawback, from both the recruiter's and the candidate's point of view, is the lack of visual feedback during the conversation. These subtle, visual clues to how well we are doing are denied us, so we must be focused and alert to picking up on purely verbal indications. If the interviewer is good at what they do, they will have prepared well at their end and the call will have a clear structure and purpose. This is good for you as it stops the conversation straying into areas which may have pitfalls in them for you.

In your responses, try to be clear and concise. Remember that the reason a telephone interview is happening in the first place is to speed up the whole recruitment process, so highly detailed, long-winded answers are not called for here. I would also suggest that you make sure that your diction is good so the interviewer understands you clearly. If anything, slow down your speech slightly to allow extra time for the interviewer to make written notes about what you are saying. If you don't have shorthand skills and have ever tried to capture people's words verbatim, you will know exactly how difficult that is! Do what works for you. Some people have found that standing up during a telephone interview helps them focus (no opportunity to doodle) and helps with their breathing and posture. This translates into sounding composed over the telephone.

You may want to rehearse beforehand. Try writing your own set of questions and have someone telephone you and ask you these questions. Remember that this is unlikely to be the hiring stage, so the questions are unlikely to be complex or demanding. Get them to write down your responses and add their own critique. Analyse these notes and amend your approach accordingly.

Part of the purpose of the telephone interview, from the recruiter's perspective, is to find out how much you want the job and (in the case of sales jobs) whether you have closing skills.

As soon as it seems appropriate during the conversation, ask for a date to meet for a face-to-face interview. Say something like: 'Well, this certainly sounds like just the job I'm looking for, Mr X. I'm sure I can contribute a lot to your organisation. I'd really like to visit you to show you what I can offer. When and where would you meet me?'

You may have to be content with the response: 'Well, we have a few other candidates to talk to yet, but we will be in touch', but at the very least you can ask "When am I likely to hear from you?". If the manager umms and ahhs, decide upon a reasonable timescale, and suggest 'Well, I'm very keen to know if I'm going forward to the next stage, so if I haven't heard from you by next Friday, would you mind if I call you then for find out?' This approach is particularly important if you are applying for sales jobs, as you are expected to demonstrate your natural salesmanship. But even in the case of other jobs, most people will appreciate your keenness and enthusiasm. If they don't, and you lose the job on account of being 'too pushy' (most unlikely), well, is it the sort of job you wanted anyway?

If after a telephone interview you don't get called to the next stage, do not be afraid to contact the recruiter again and ask for feedback on your performance. This will help you to improve your own skills and hopefully produce a more positive outcome in the future.

CHAPTER 10

FURTHER TYPICAL INTERVIEW QUESTIONS

Earlier in the book you had the opportunity to see the kinds of answers that interviewers are really looking for. However, there are a million and one other subjects that you could be asked questions on, and I have included here just a selection for you to look at. This is like an exam: you may broadly know what will be covered, but not the actual questions. As you look at them, try and formulate the type of answer you would give to each one using the guidelines previously provided.

DRIVE FOR ACHIEVEMENT

Seizes opportunities to achieve and exceed both business and personal objectives.

Q Tell us about a time when you have been especially motivated.

- What most strongly motivates you to work hard?
- How does this show itself?
- What demotivates you?

Q Tell us about a time when you worked especially hard

- Which aspects of the situation motivated you to work hard?
- Which aspect of the situation demotivated you?
- What feedback did you receive on your performance?

Q Describe a recent opportunity when you had to take on new responsibilities?

- How did the opportunity arise?
- What were these new responsibilities?
- What was the outcome?

Q Give an example of when you have set yourself an ambitious target.

- What made it so ambitious?
- How did it compare with other targets you had set yourself?
- How well did you do?

Q Describe a situation in which you had to work under pressure.

- What was the cause of the pressure?
- How did you feel under this pressure?
- What impact did this have on your work?

Q Tell me about a crisis you have handled recently.

- What caused it?
- What did you do to resolve it?
- What were your feelings at the time?

Q Tell us about a time when you felt that you were unfairly criticised.

- Why was this?
- How did you respond?
- What was the outcome?

Q Describe a situation at work when something was causing you to feel negative.

- What caused these feelings?
- How did you approach your work at the time?
- What impact did this have on your colleagues?

Q Can you tell us about a time when your drive and determination inspired others to give more commitment to their work?

- What did you say?
- How did other people respond?
- What was the result?

STRATEGIC THINKING

Able to take a broad view of industry, its threats and opportunities, and use them to identify areas of business potential that can be exploited.

Q Tell me about a recent time when you took a broad view of your own work.

- Why was this necessary?
- How useful was this approach?
- What wider implications became apparent?

Q How do you think the role for which you are applying will impact on the long-term success of the company?

- How do you see your contribution?

Q What do you know of this company's long-term strategy?

- What do you think of this strategy?
- How sensible do you think it is?

Q Give an example of a time when you could have taken a more long-term view on a project/strategy.

- Why was this important?
- What was the outcome?
- What did you learn?

RELATIONSHIP BUILDING
Puts sustained effort into building influential relationships.

Q Give me an example of a time when someone came to you for support or guidance.

- Why did they need your support?
- What did you do to support/guide them?
- How did it help?

Q Describe a time when you had to establish an effective relationship quickly.

- What did you do?
- What was the outcome?
- What did you learn from this?

Q In what past situations have you been most effective in building and maintaining relationships with others?

- What did you specifically do that was effective?

Q In which situations have you been least effective in building and maintaining relationships with others?

- What did you do that detracted from effectiveness?
- What would you have done differently?

Q What can you do to become more effective in this competency?

- What behaviours could you demonstrate more/less?

COMMERCIAL AWARENESS
Recognises how businesses work, and understands and applies commercial and financial principles.

Q What do you know about this company?

- How did you find this out?
- How would you keep this knowledge up to date?

Q What do you know about the competitors in this business?

- What are the key strengths of their strategy?
- How do you think we could we be more successful?
- What opportunities do you see for growing the business in this area?

Q Why, in your opinion, do customers choose our products and services?

- What benefits do they have for the customer?
- How could we make them more competitive?
- How could we make them more profitable?
- What are the market trends that affect us?

Q In what way do you think the role for which you are applying contributes to our overall business performance?

- How could we measure this impact?

Q What is the most important thing you have done to take account of costs/profits/commercial value?

- What prompted you?

■ What long-term impact did you have?

■ How could you have increased this further?

Q Give an example of a time when you spotted a good business opportunity.

■ What was this?

■ Why did you think it was worthwhile?

■ What was the outcome?

Q What general commercial factors do you think are most critical in managing the financial performance of any area of business?

■ How commercial is your outlook compared to your peers?

■ How do you know?

■ What do you perceive to be your biggest commercial failure? Why?

LEADERSHIP OF CHANGE

Identifies ways to improve our business. Engages with all colleagues to support them through ambiguity and transition.

Q **Describe an occasion when you had to change the way you work because of changing circumstances.**

- What were the main changes in terms of demands?
- What was your initial reaction?
- How well did you adapt?

Q **Give an example of a time when you had to change your work plans unexpectedly.**

- What was your first reaction?
- How did you change your plans?
- What was the outcome?

Q **Describe a time when you needed to explain to colleagues an unexpected change in work plans.**

- What was their reaction?
- How did you manage their adaptation?

Q **Suggestions for change often come from the unlikeliest of sources. Tell us about a time when this has happened to you.**

- What was the catalyst for change?
- What was your reaction?
- How did you manage your colleagues' reactions?
- What was the outcome?

Q Give us a recent example of when you came up with a different approach/solution to a situation or problem.

- What suggestions did you make?
- Which ideas were put into practice?
- What was the outcome?

Q Describe a crisis at work that you have had to handle recently.

- What caused it?
- What did you do to resolve it?

Q In what past situations have you been most effective at motivating others through periods of change?

- What did you do specifically that was effective?
- What supportive conditions were present?

Q Think of someone who's particularly effective in motivating others – what do they do exactly?

LEADERSHIP SKILLS
Creates and communicates a compelling vision and sense of purpose.

Q Describe a time when your input motivated others to reach a team goal.

- Why was this necessary?
- What did you do to motivate the team?
- Why did this work?

Q Describe a time when you successfully helped someone to carry out a task independently.

- How did you enable them to carry out the work?
- How did you follow this up?
- What was the outcome?

Q Describe a situation when you found it difficult to focus the work of a team on an objective.

- What made this work difficult?
- How did you try to overcome these difficulties?
- How could you improve upon this?

Q What opportunities have you had to identify development opportunities for others?

- What action did you take?
- Why was this important?
- What impact did this have?

Q We all have times when we find it difficult to control the activities of others. Give an example of when you faced this type of situation.

- Why did you find the situation challenging?
- How did you overcome the difficulties you faced?

Q In what past situations have you been most effective in providing leadership and direction?

- What did you specifically do that was effective?
- What supportive conditions were present?
- In which situations were you least effective?
- What could you have done differently?

Q In what situations have you been most effective in empowering others?

- What did you do that was especially effective?
- What results did you see?

CONTINUOUS IMPROVEMENT

Identifies the processes needed to make things happen in a quality-oriented way and to get things actioned.

Q Tell us about a time when you have had to identify the key cause of a problem.

- What processes did you adopt to identify the key cause?
- How did you solve the problem?
- What lessons did you learn?

Q Tell us about a situation where you have implemented a process that you didn't initially agree with.

Q Describe the last time you had to analyse a lot of information or data.

- What sort of information did this involve?
- How did you pick out the essential information from the less relevant?
- What did you learn from the analysis?

Q Give us a recent example of when you were faced with a complex problem.

- What made it complex?
- What key steps did you take to resolve the problem?
- What did others think of your approach?

Q **Most people have potentially experienced situations where they wished they had taken action to deal with an issue sooner. When have you anticipated a potential problem like this?**

- How did you identify the problem?
- What steps did you take to address it?
- What feedback did you receive?

Q **Describe a time when you had to organise the implementation of a new process/plan or project.**

- What key stages did you work through?
- On what basis did you determine your priorities?
- How did this work out in practice?

Q **Even the most organised individuals may find that they overlook some of the activities required in planning new activities/initiatives. Tell us about a time when this happened to you.**

- What were the consequences of this?
- How did you rectify this?
- What was the outcome?

Q **Give an example of when you had to organise a piece of work, project or event.**

- How did you prepare and plan for it?
- What timescales did you set?
- How well did it go?

Q Give an example of when you had to work to an important deadline.

- How manageable were your timescales?
- What did you do to ensure that the deadline was met?
- What did you learn?

Q Describe the last time you missed a deadline. Why did this happen?

CUSTOMER AWARENESS

Dedicated to meeting and exceeding the expectations and requirements of all customers.

Q How much contact have you had with customers?

- What do you like about dealing with them?
- What do you dislike?

Q Give an example of when you put a customer first.

- What sacrifices did you have to make?
- What impact did this have on your other activities?
- How did others view this?

Q Tell me about the last time a customer made an excessive or unreasonable demand on you.

- What made them so demanding?
- What did you do to assist them?
- How much time did this take?

Q Tell me about a time when you have kept your promise to a customer, even though it was really tough.

Q Describe a time when you were unable to help out a customer as much as they wanted.

- Why was this?
- What did they say about your reaction?
- What did your manager say?

Q Tell me about a time when you were complimented for helping a customer beyond the call of duty.

- How frequently do you go to that kind of trouble?
- What other similar feedback have you received?
- What feedback have you had from colleagues?

Q Give an example of a time when you had to listen very carefully to a customer.

- What did they tell you?
- How did you check you had grasped all the information?
- How did you show you were listening?

Q Describe a situation in which you have had to deal with a particularly angry customer

- Why were they angry?
- How did you begin to calm them down?
- What would you do differently?

Q What do you think are the key factors that influence a customer's first impression?

- Why do you think they are important?

DECISION-MAKING SKILLS AND JUDGEMENT

Demonstrates a readiness to make quality decisions based on logical analysis of information, and can originate action.

Q In what past situations have you shown sound judgement?

- What did you do specifically that was effective?

Q Think of someone who shows excellent judgement – what do they do exactly?

Q Describe the last time you had to make a spur-of-the-moment decision.

- Why was this necessary?
- How did your decision affect others?
- What consequences had you not considered?

Q Tell us about a time when you took responsibility for making a key decision.

- What was your decision?
- How did you defend your decision?
- What was the possible impact of a poor decision?

Q Describe a time when you referred a decision upwards.

- What was the background?
- Why did you need help?
- To what extent do you seek advice?

Q Tell us about a recent situation in which you had to be totally objective when reaching a decision.

- What were the facts you had to review?
- How did you weight the different pieces of information?
- Looking back, what do you think of your decision?

Q How would you describe your preferred style of making judgements?

- What are the key strengths of this?
- How does this compare with your colleagues' style?

Q How would you describe your preferred style of making decisions?

- Where do you typically source your information?

Q We all have to make unpopular decisions that may affect others. Describe a situation when you have had to make such a decision.

- Why did you take it?
- How did the people who were affected react?
- What did you learn from this experience?

Q Can you tell us about a time when you had to source information from a variety of sources and make business judgements based upon it?

- Talk us through the actual steps you took in this process.

INFLUENCING SKILLS

Influences, convinces or impresses others in a way that results in acceptance, agreement or behaviour change.

Q Tell me about the last time that you won someone over to your point of view.

- How did your opinion contrast with their original position?
- What were the key things that you did which persuaded them?
- What kind of agreement did you reach?

Q Give a recent example of when you negotiated a successful outcome.

- What did you negotiate?
- How did you win the person round?
- How did you know that they were really convinced?

Q Give an example of a time when you were unable to persuade someone round to your point of view.

- Why was this important?
- Why did you not succeed?
- What have you learnt?

Q There are times when no one is prepared to listen or agree with a point of view. Give an example of when this happened to you.

- How did you present your view/idea?
- What were their objections?
- How hard did you push your viewpoint?
- Where did you leave the conversation?

Q **For most of us, the occasion arises when we must convince others to make an unpopular choice/decision. Give an example of when you have had to do this.**

- How did you try to get others on board?
- What was the result?
- With hindsight, how could you have approached this differently?

Q **What kind of correspondence/presentations have you had to produce in the past?**

- How frequently have you had to write this kind of work?
- How was it received?
- Did people/colleagues understand what you had said?

Q **Tell me about your experience in preparing reports/documents.**

- How often have you had to prepare reports?
- How do you go about it?
- What do you do particularly well?

Q **For many businesses good communication is key for success. What factors, in your view, ensure good communication?**

- What advice might you give to someone struggling with his or her communication?
- How might you improve your own written communication?
- What steps have you taken to do this?

Q In what situations do you find it difficult to get your point across?

- Why is this so?
- What do you do to overcome these difficulties?
- What methods have you observed others use?

Q Think of one of your colleagues who you consider to be very influential. How does your style differ from theirs?

- Give an example of your approach.

Q Tell us about a situation when you had to modify your plans/actions to take account of other people's views.

- What was the situation?
- How did the other people express their views?

Q How do you get your boss/others to accept an idea?

DEVELOPMENT OF SELF AND OTHERS

Has the ability, and interest, to take responsibility for own development and to support and coach the development of others.

Q What can you do to become more effective in developing other people?

■ What behaviours should you practise more/less?

Q Where are you most effective in attracting and developing the talent of others?

Q In what situations have you succeeded in furthering your own personal development?

■ How did you do this?
■ What risks did you take?

Q Tell me about a situation where you felt you failed in your own personal development.

■ Why do you think it happened?
■ What have you learned from this?

Q Describe a recent opportunity you had to take on new responsibilities.

■ How did the opportunity arise?
■ What were the new responsibilities?
■ What was the outcome?

Q When was the last time you learned a new skill (at work)?

- What was it?
- How did you apply your learning?
- What feedback did you receive about your performance?

Q What example can you give us where you have supported and encouraged a colleague?

- What did you do?
- What did they need?
- What was the result?

Q Describe a situation in which you have been faced with a difficult individual.

- How did you handle this?

Q Describe how your current role has changed/developed over the years.

Q Tell me about your professional style, how it has developed/changed over the years.

- Has there been a time when it was inappropriate and you had to adapt it?

Q Give us an example of a time when you were unfairly criticised about something.

- Why was this?
- How did you respond?
- What was the outcome?

TEAMWORKING SKILLS
Works cooperatively and productively with all colleagues.

Q In what past situations have you been most effective as a teamworker?

- What did you specifically do that was effective?

Q In which situations were you least effective as a teamworker?

- What did you do that detracted from effectiveness?
- What could you have done differently?

Q Think of someone who's a particularly effective team player – what do they do exactly?

Q What makes a supportive team?

- Why do you think this is important?
- What can be done to encourage people to work together more supportively?
- What gets in the way of successful teamworking?

SPECIALIST KNOWLEDGE

Has the appropriate background knowledge and expertise and understands technical or professional aspects of work.

Q How do you keep up with advances in your profession?

- How much time do you spend doing this?
- Which specialist or technical magazines or journals do you read?
- How do your efforts to keep up with developments compare with those of your peers?

Q Tell me about a time when colleagues sought your technical advice or experience.

- Why do you think they sought your advice?
- How accurate was your advice?
- What have you done since to acquire extra knowledge?

Q Which technical problems are the most challenging for you?

- What are your strengths and weaknesses technically?
- How does your level of knowledge compare with that of your peers?
- What feedback have you received about it?

Q What methods do you choose to learn by and why do you prefer these?

Q Give an example of when your technical/specialist knowledge helped you to solve a problem.

- What brought this issue to light?
- What did you do?
- What was the result of your efforts?

Q Describe a recent occasion when you felt that your level of specialist knowledge was insufficient.

- What made you think this?
- What action did you take?
- What are your current strengths and weaknesses in this area?

Q It can sometimes be difficult to apply the knowledge gained in specialised courses to the workplace. What opportunities have you had to do this?

- How did you adapt the knowledge?
- What was the outcome?

Q What steps do you take to apply your specialist knowledge to a commercial environment?

- How useful is that approach?
- What are the limitations of that approach?

Q Give an example of an area where you would consider yourself to have detailed knowledge or expertise.

- Tell me what important changes are taking place in this field.
- What are the implications of this?

Q What sort of professional standards have you had to adhere to in the past?

- Why were they important?
- What difficulties did you encounter maintaining them?
- How did you ensure that others also complied with these standards?

APPENDIX: THE JOKE'S ON HR

As a member of a minority group (HR professionals) I feel I can relate to you some funny stories where HR is the butt of the joke without fear of reprisal from the politically correct brigade. These are just a few jokes I have picked up along the way. Enjoy.

Q: How many HR managers does it take to change a light bulb?
A: Only one, but he reserves the right to take his time about it as the company would need to be aware of the light bulb's view on change and also the view of the other stakeholders involved.

Once upon a time there was a shepherd looking after his flock of sheep on a back road in deepest Wales. Just then, a shiny BMW screeched to a halt beside him and the passenger leans out the window and says to the shepherd: 'If I can guess how many sheep you have, can I keep one?'

The shepherd says, 'Right you are then.'

The woman in the car connects her laptop to a mobile phone, logs into the NASA website, scans the field using a satellite, opens a database linked to 142 Excel files filled with formulae, logarithms, pivot and look-up tables, then prints out a 100-page report on a 12-volt DC-powered micro printer. She says to the shepherd 'You have 1398 sheep exactly.'

'That's right. You can take your pick of my flock' says the shepherd.

The woman packs all her gear up, looks at the flock, picks one up and shoves it in the boot. As she is about to leave the shepherd says, 'If I can guess what you do for a living, will you give my animal back to me?'

The woman agrees and the shepherd says 'You're an HR manager'.

'That's amazing', cried the woman. 'How did you know?'

'First of all, you came here without being invited. Second of all you spent ages telling me what I already knew. And finally you don't understand a thing about what I do, but interfered anyway. Now, can I have my bloody dog back?'

An HR manager sadly passed away and her soul drifted up to the Pearly Gates where St Peter stood to welcome her.

'We've never had an HR manager make it this far before. We're not really sure what to do with you, so the Boss has said we've to give you one day in Hell and one day in Heaven and then let you choose where you want to stay for eternity.'

'Oh then, I choose Heaven' said the woman.

'Not so fast', said St Peter. 'You must experience both before you make your choice', and puts the woman on the downward escalator to Hell.

As the doors opened in Hell, the woman stepped out into a beautiful garden. In the distance was a rose-framed cottage; around her were many friends, all with smiling faces. They ran up to her and kissed and hugged her and welcomed her and they chatted about old times. They had a lovely afternoon together and rounded off their day with a beautiful a la carte dinner washed down with the finest champagne. Just as she was getting really into the swing of things it was time to leave. Everyone hugged her and waved her off as she set off up the escalator towards the Pearly Gates.

St Peter was waiting for her once more and said, 'Now its time to spend a day in Heaven', and off she went on the up escalator to Heaven.

For the next 24 hours the HR manager spent all her time lolling around on clouds, plucking her harp and preening her wings and singing sweetly, all of which was just about as pleasant as her time in Hell.

At the end of her day, St Peter returned and said to her, 'You've spent a day in Heaven and a day in Hell. Now you must choose which one where you will spend eternity'.

The woman thought for a bit then said, 'Well Heaven's nice, of course, but actually I had a better time in Hell, so I think I'll choose Hell'.

The woman was dispatched down the escalator to Hell but when she got there this time there before her stood a desolate wasteland, with stinking piles of rubbish and the people were wailing and full of sorrow.

At that, the devil popped up and put his arm round her shoulder. 'Everything OK?' he said.

'I don't understand', the HR manager stammered. 'When I was here before everything was wonderful, we ate fantastic food and everyone was happy'.

'Ahh' said the Devil 'When you were here before we were recruiting. Now you are staff...'

The following represents (allegedly) true comments made by line managers on employees' annual appraisal forms:

- Since my last report, this employee has reached rock bottom and has started to dig.

- I would not allow this employee to breed.
- This employee is really not so much of a has-been but more of a definite won't-be.
- Works well when under constant supervision and cornered like a rat in a trap.
- When she opens her mouth, it seems that it is only to change feet.
- He would be out of his depth in a parking lot puddle.
- This young lady has delusions of adequacy.
- He sets low personal standards and then consistently fails to achieve them.
- This employee is depriving a village somewhere of an idiot.
- This employee should go far, and the sooner he starts, the better.
- Got a full six-pack but lacks the plastic thing to hold it all together.
- A gross ignoramus – 144 times worse than an ordinary ignoramus.
- He does not have ulcers, but he is a carrier.
- I would like to go hunting with him sometime.
- He has been working with glue too much.
- He would argue with a signpost.
- He brings a lot of joy whenever he leaves the room.
- When his IQ reaches 50, he should sell.
- If you see two people talking, and one looks bored, he is the other one.
- A photographic memory but with the lens covered glued on.
- A prime candidate for natural de-selection.
- Donated his brain to science before he was done using it.
- Gates are down, the lights are flashing but the train is not coming.
- Has two brains: one is lost and the other is out looking for it.
- If he were any more stupid, he would have to be watered twice a week.
- If you give him a penny for his thoughts, you would get change.
- If you stand close enough to him, you can hear the ocean.
- It is hard to believe that he beat out 1,000,000 other sperm.
- One neuron short of a synapse.

- Some drink from the fountain of knowledge; he only gargled.
- Takes him two hours to watch 60 minutes.
- The wheel is turning, but the hamster is dead.

INDEX OF QUESTIONS

QUESTIONS ABOUT YOUR DRIVE FOR ACHIEVEMENT
Tell me what you know about our business?

Give an example of when you've experienced a setback.

What have you done to progress your education to date?

QUESTIONS ABOUT YOUR STRATEGIC THINKING
In what past situations have you shown most evidence of visionary/strategic thinking?

What do you see as the main threats to our business in the long-term? What can we do to ensure long-term success?

QUESTIONS ABOUT YOUR RELATIONSHIP BUILDING
Tell me about a recent situation when you had to build a relationship with a new colleague. Why was the relationship important?

Think of someone who's particularly effective at building and maintaining relationships with others. What do they do exactly?

How do you behave when you meet new people?

QUESTIONS ABOUT YOUR CONTINUOUS IMPROVEMENT
Tell us about a time when you initiated an improvement at work.

Tell us about how you normally cope with a lot of work.

- Where do you start?
- What do you do to ensure it all gets done?
- What prevents you from getting it all done?

QUESTIONS ON YOUR LEADERSHIP OF CHANGE

Tell us about a recent time when you had to adapt to a major change

- How did you adapt?
- What was difficult about the transition?

Tell us about a time when you questioned or challenged a way of working.

- Why did you question it?
- What alternative did you suggest?
- To what extent were your ideas used?

QUESTIONS ABOUT YOUR LEADERSHIP SKILLS

Describe a time when you had to coordinate the work of other people.

- What were you trying to achieve?
- How did you go about organising the work?

Think of someone who is particularly effective in providing leadership. What do you think they do successfully?

QUESTIONS ABOUT YOUR CUSTOMER AWARENESS

What, in your view, makes it difficult to relate well to certain customers?

Tell me about a recent situation when you had to build a relationship with a new customer.

Give me an example when you have given excellent customer service.

QUESTIONS ABOUT YOUR INFLUENCING SKILLS
What are your strengths in terms of influencing people?

- What's your approach in influencing others?
- What could you do to make yourself more effective in influencing others?

Give an example of when you had to settle a dispute between two people.

Have you ever had a conflict with a superior? How was it resolved?

Some people are easier to persuade than others. Which people do you find it hard to persuade?

- What is it that makes persuading them so difficult?

QUESTIONS ABOUT YOUR DEVELOPMENT OF SELF AND OTHERS
What do you consider to be your weaknesses?

What would you consider to be your development needs?

In what past situations have you been most effective in developing others?

What did you do specifically that was effective?

What was the last piece of learning you undertook?

QUESTIONS ABOUT YOUR TEAM WORKING SKILLS
Tell us about the last time you worked as part of a team.

- What did you like about working in the group?
- What did you dislike?

Tell me about a time when you had to get people to work together more supportively.

- What caused the original difficulties?
- How did the others respond to you?
- What would you do differently next time?

QUESTIONS ABOUT YOUR DECISION-MAKING SKILLS AND JUDGEMENT

Tell us about a recent situation in which you had to reach a decision without having all the facts.

How do you usually go about solving a problem?

Would you say you are good at making decisions?

QUESTIONS ABOUT YOUR COMMERCIAL AWARENESS

Why, in your opinion, do customers choose our products and services?

How could we make them more competitive?

What are the market trends that affect us?

What opportunities have you had to identify cost savings in the past? Give an example.

How did you choose where to make the savings?

How much money do you think you saved?

INDEX